1

ICE PELLETS

Collection of intuitive thoughts

- Joseph Leonardo

TABLE OF CONTENTS

PREFACE BY THE AUTHOR

Human thoughts are like rain drops that keep falling from the sky. As children, we pick up these drops of water falling from the sky and store them or drink them when necessary. I still remember, I was in a particular village, it was towards the evening, during the whole morning, the light from the sun has tortured the earth, and it was during the evening time, approximately after 4, few drops of rain started falling down to cool the earth. With the rain, I could see Ice pellets falling to the ground. I saw kids running in the rain to collect those Ice pellets. They have gathered them and placed them in their hands and waiting until they are melted away completely. It is estimated that on an average, every person has 6,200 thoughts per day, running across the mind, good, bad, positive and negative thoughts, about life, social, family, religion, and so on. I would always considered them like diamonds, must collect them like children collecting Ice pellets and savor and preserve them for our use for our future reference.

Here, in this book, I have collected some of my thoughts over the years and put them together, in order to help my readers.

Joseph Leonardo

Our expectations from a movie

Movies are basically elements and bits and pieces of fiction, gathered and collected from imagination of human mind. We basically live in a harsh world. Movie is like an utopia where everyone wants to make an escape for at least a few hours and forget our surroundings. A movie does give us a hope, desire, entertainment, knowledge, etc….. to live on…….. the strongest clinging element is HOPE. It creates a world of fantasy, lovely place, and creates supernatural elements, and the list goes on. Usually, everyone goes to a theater, just to relax, that is why, whenever we have a festival or weekends or on Sundays, these are the important days on which we prefer to go to theaters and spend some time in theater to relax and forgot our world.

In the ancient days, dramas were most popular form of entertainment and people used to rush to auditoriums to watch dramas, but thank god for the invention of light technology today and we are able to visualize with much more graphical appearance in the form of light on silver screens. It is more colorful and we are able to create a new world with mesmerizing music that can take us into different world of beings. Movies are stories, stories of different people, different situations, of places, of heroic figures, and/or fiction that are being created with lots of imagination and creativity. There are so many sorts of literary genres, which serve the purpose of everyone, some are fond of romantic movies, some are fond of horror, action, comedy, and so on. These days, these literary genres are being mixed like cocktail, and yet, we are able to experience new kind of experience through those genres.

As human beings, we all go through life differently, we all have different kinds of experiences, because that is how we were born. Stories have different impact on different classes of people. Higher classes and educated people have different tastes when it comes to stories, youth will have different taste and are more attracted to love tracks and horror tracks because of their age and it gives them thrill and enjoyment in those genres. Some uneducated people would wish some action sequences while some might like sentimental movies, and thus, different sets of people have their own expectations about watching movies.

Among the major genres, here, are the list of some genes and they are as follows;

Dramas, thriller, horror, horror comedy, romance, fiction, science fiction, history, biography, historical figures, action, action comedy, psychological thrillers, war movies, epic movies, fantasy, sentimental movies, emotions, and so on, the list goes on.

Expectations: In the olden days, whenever the movie is being released, people used to rush to watch the movie and the same movie would run for nearly 100 to 200 days. Number of people who used to go to theater were more when compared to today. The reason being, there was not much technology at homes, like for example, no television sets to watch any programs. So, watching on white screen was something amazing for everyone in the form of light and sound and it gave a great amusement and thrill. This is why, whatever movie came to theater, it would run minimum of 50 days without fail, but today, things are different, just hardly a week to two week if the movie is very good or a month. None of us have authority to judge a movie because no movie makers will make or intent to make bad movies, everybody will put lot of efforts in making good movies only.

Generally speaking, all movies are very good, they come up with good story and concept, perhaps, and presentation of a movie might falter, but not fail completely. Now, when it comes to, lets says, why some people say, some movies are good, some movies are average, some movies are below average. These kinds of reviews come from the minds of people. I wish to give an example here, lets says, I have organized a trip or picnic to some beautiful place and taken around 10 people with me for a couple of days and the trip was bit expensive. Now, everything went well, I believed that everyone enjoyed the trip. So, decided to take the review, but out of ten people, only two people liked the place, but why. We all decided about the place and went ahead with everyone's consent and in spite of that, only two people liked and place and only few enjoyed the time. It is not that place is bad or time is bad. Each one has different taste and no one has authority to force some one's wishes and likes on them just because I spent so much money to organize the trip. Suppose, I like chicken curry and I do not presume that you should like the chicken curry, and you may also like the chicken curry, but perhaps, you did not like the way it is being prepared. Here, the underlying reason lies, the preparation, how it is being prepared, that is also very important and plays a very important role.

So, in the same way, when it comes to movies, perhaps, I might like the movie or someone cannot force me to like the movie and I believe, I am expecting more from the movie or it is not being prepared or executed properly as per my opinion. Usually speaking, there is so much thought goes into movie planning and execution part, but somewhere down the line, something will still be missing and this happens since we are all human.

Pattern of thinking: As human beings, each one has different thought patterns. Each of us have different believe systems, opinion sets, thought patterns, which cannot be changed so easily. Each one form this thinking pattern and learns from the society and some change their thinking pattern down the line and as they grow up and are bit flexible, and hence, they are broad minded people. Narrow minded people are such, they stick to certain kind of thinking and are not willing to change their thinking, even though it does not suit the contemporary thought pattern. Now, when it comes to movies, suppose, a new movie is being released today, irrespective of any genre, usually, many people go to that movie to watch with certain amount of expectation and for the sake of their hero. Here, the main problem lies, if the story goes according to their expectations, then it is a successful movie. Here, another element is about the hero also, when it comes to action movies, no one should beat the hero, and audience will not accept and digest that fact. Suppose, if the movie story is not to their expectations, then, it's bad movie.

So, here, the burning fact is that audience decides whether movie is good or bad, but the main question one should ask is, is everyone watching the movie with broad mind or without expecting anything from the movie. Any movie in particular, whenever you go to watch the movie, watch the story without expecting anything irrespective of your favorite star. Hence, I believe, we must watch any movie without any expectations, watch it, considering and expecting a new story, new twists, new food in a new dish and do not think of any particular hero. So, if one tries to watch the movie without any expectations, then, I believe every movie has something to offer us, something to teach us, some new knowledge to hand over to us, although at times, preparation may be a bit weak, but every movie is a good movie.

What do movies showcase

Movies are visual representations of images, sounds, light, graphical appearance and that is why, they are so appealing and they attract us. Movies, movies, movies, oh god, it has a great impact on our lives, even small kids today are attracted to the movies, videos etc. Movies give us a great delight and happiness. Movies is a holiday spot and a picnic spot on weekends or on Sundays, and especially on festive days, movie is a must. During holiday season, it's a main adda (area or place) for everyone. We will not and cannot afford to miss any single movie during these holiday season.

Movies hypnotize us: Movies hypnotize us and for instance, we have gone to the theater and sit in the theater, watching the movie. During the whole process of the movie, we completely focus on the movie itself only. We get so engrossed and involved in the movie if the movie is very interesting. Movie is always so captivating and captures our minds and we cannot even think of moving out of the chairs and relaxing. Movie in fact has dominion over us during those couple of hours. It tells us what to do and what not to do. It happens not only in theaters, but when you are outside, have come out of the theater, the same music, sounds, pictures, images keep ringing in our ears and in our minds and it will not go away until a few days until we get involved deeply in our daily routine and in our work. We even go to the extent of doing some research on that particular subject because it has made such an impact on us and we cannot even forget about those events of the movie.

Movies give us knowledge: Movies are nothing, but mingled with great elements. Movie means, it is a beautiful story narrated well and presented in the form of light and sound. Movies give us knowledge, they teach us so many things. They are educational and these days, in majority of the schools and colleges, movies are being played for educational purpose. Students watch them in order to learn something, about some place or about great events or some documentaries, which furnishes with further education. We can learn so many things from movies, new knowledge, new mannerisms, language, how each one behaves in each situation. It gives us lot of ideas to deal with difficult situations, helps us to sought out many issues. Some of the educational movies are like school of life, freedom writers, the class, inside job, teachers, etc, list goes on.

They make us believe that something is true and real: Movies are so captivating and they hypnotize our minds. They make us believe, oh god, really... that is why, some people ask after watching movie when new things are displayed in the movie, is it really true. They leave such puzzling queries in the minds of people. Many people believe every movie to be a true story, especially uneducated people.

They take us to different worlds: Fantasy movies take us to different worlds. As kid, perhaps, everyone like to be and love to listen stories of fantasy and that something is not real, but they are of course, very interesting stories. Aladdin, Cinderella, aquaman, maleficent etc.. are some of the examples of the fantasy movies. Aquaman is a movie where life is projected in the ocean and it is really unimaginable that human like life can exist in water.

Animated movies: Today, since the evolution of technology, we are able to movie so many animated movies. It was such a laborious job to build and make animated movies, but today, it is really very easy task. These days, not only kids, but on a normal scenario, all of us are able to watch animated movies and would love watching animated movies because they are so interesting. These kinds of stories take us to another level and there is so much to laugh about from these movies.

They limit our thinking: Yes, they limit our thinking, and I am still wondering as why so many horror movies are being made and in every horror movie, the same concept lies, possessed by a ghost, a person who has died some time back and has come to take revenge. I really cannot understand, whey these movies keep projecting the same thing again and again, making people believe, even though it is not truth. How can a ghost or spirit take possession of another body. It does not make any sense and it's not logical either. Suppose, for example, take an empty glass and fill it with water to the brim, now, consider this full glass to be yourself and your soul.

Now, let us say, the so called ghost, an outer element has come to possess you, and take another glass of water and try to pour into the glass, which is already full to the brim and is there any scope to take in any more water and if you try to pour it also, water will be spilled out and cannot take it. In that case, how can a ghost enter your body where already, soul exists in that body unless that present soul is removed completed and for that to happen, that person has to go through the process of death, but even then, the external element called ghost cannot enter, because every human body consists of energy chakras.

This human body and chakras cannot and will not accept new external force to enter into your body. Human body cannot accept foreign elements, that is why, when people experience cancer, kidney stones, etc.., they experience excruciating pain because these are external materials and body does not like it to have within the body that is why it reacts in the form of severe pain. This is only one example, I wish to give and there are of course, many other things that limit our thinking.

The power of positive thinking

We are living in a world of material which, which is tangible. We can touch, feel and experience all that we see. There is a great energy that drives behind this physical force and that I would call is energy. In this world, we are faced with both positive elements as well as with negative elements. Positive energetic elements always give us joy, peace and happiness whereas negative energy through negative people gives us unhappiness and makes our lives miserable. There is an element of positivity and negativity in all of us, but how do we handle with negativity is the biggest question that comes to us. Hence, lets us discuss further the details and the ways as to how to face this negativity and overcome it with a smile.

Life is short, so, smile while you still have teeth. Perhaps, this is said in a humorous way, but there is an element of truth in it. We should always be happy in whichever circumstances we may be. The positive element is always within us and hence, we must use this positive energy always rather than negative energy. Life is always full of happiness and we are never dressed fully without a proper smile, so, wear a smile and after all, we will not lose anything and in fact, we will get bright smiles in return. If you notice something, try to give a smile and say hello to anyone and the moment you say that, you will notice that certain positive energy gets transferred from that person to you and vice versa. So, do not you think, it's really amazing, and yes, indeed, it's truly amazing. So, it's better to stay positive.

Gives us good health: being happy is the secret of good health. Suppose, if one is always moody and gets concerned and worried all the time or angry all the time, then, lot of miseries keep creeping in one's life as a result of this negative energy. Energy is like fire particles, which we cannot see, which flows continuously throughout our body with and without our knowledge. If we invite positive energy, then, that is fine, or else, we this energy particle will have great reaction to our human mechanism, kind of, can upset stomach, cause anxiety, fear, etc.. so, why should we give that opportunity to negative energy. Moreover, by being angry on someone, we do not gain anything and in fact, we are holding that negative energy within us and not letting it go. So, the secret to true happiness and health is to let go of that negative force and invite positive energy within us and thus, we can wear a true smile on our face as well as be happy within.

Negligent parents: I will give one good example, one person is born in a poor family. He/she has been struggling throughout life with no proper food and on the other hand, he has grown up with ill-treatment by his father. Here, the biggest problem is, basically speaking, every child, from the moment he is born into any family, tries to learn from the surroundings, especially he will pick up basic knowledge about life from his parents first. In other words, the kid has been experiencing tough life since his childhood and never received any rewards from his father or mother or from any of his relatives or society or friends. So, he will be under the impression that the world is very bad and, as a result of it, he has picked up lot of negative vibrations throughout his life. So, in life, when he grows up, he always grows to be a negative person only. In other words, positive elements cannot enter into his life unless he encounters with someone who will be very sweet later on in his life.

Spirituality: We always believe, that spiritually plays only a part in everyone's life, and it's not necessary at all, but being spiritual is very essential if we have to develop positive energy. It is the spirit that helps us and guides us to become a better person. Now, in the case of above person, he will definitely have a scope to develop positive energy and lead good life later on through some form or the other. Now, being a negative person, one cannot really attract good things in life because, all our emotions, thought and intensions are all relative to some form of energy. Suppose, for example, I am waiting in the bus stand, waiting for the bus and the climate is bit hot. After some time, I start grumbling and say, its difficult to get buses in time these days. Now, what did I just say, its difficult to get buses in time these days, which means, I am cursing for the buses not to come in time. Suppose, if I say, oh, nothing to worry, perhaps, bus drivers would have gone for lunch and it will come, say it in your mind, the bus will definitely come, here, you are blessing and wishing for good thing to happen. As I mentioned earlier, every thought and emotion that comes from our minds or hearts, is a energy particle that we are throwing ahead in the future for things to happen. So, always, remember, wish for something good. These wishes and curses will disappoint us or bless us, either by other people or by ourselves.

I wish to give one more example in this regard, which I had experienced long back. After completion of graduation, I was studying one course in one of the hill stations in South India. I do not wish to give exact location due to personal reasons. Now, we were a batch of approximately 30 and the place was very good. Hill station is always beautiful and we could experience clouds passing by and touching us and we could feel the chillness as they pass by. The climate is so amazing, greenery everywhere. The air is so fresh and there is no scope of pollution. Since being hill station, there is a forest and tea estates that were present and everything was so beautiful. I would say, in one word, it's really heaven. Life in the hill station was so beautiful and so pleasant. Now, here the main problem was, sometimes, we were asked to go for trekking, which was of course, a beautiful and delightful experience. We could see some animals like deers, bisons, chita, hina, etc and would hear pleasant singing from the birds also. Of course, everything was cool, but when I looked at the ground, the ground was so wet and leaves were wet also. So, we carried sticks with us to support our walking. Here, the main problem is, whenever the forest is wet and damp, forest land will have many leeches on the ground. Coming to the point, I was scared of leeches because they crawl up on to the legs without our knowledge and we will not have pain when they get on one's body and slowly suck blood. They are rubbery creatures and will not leave human body until they get sufficient food for themselves. I was so careful while walking to make sure that none of these creatures crawl on me. I wished very strongly and these creatures should never get on to me. Surprisingly, all my classmates experienced this phenomenon of being blood sucked by these creatures many times, but for me, it never happened. I call this, the power of positive mind or positive thinking.

So, here, the point I want to make is, have a strong and positive thinking always and things will happen for anyone positively.

I wish to give another example, this incident occurred while I was teaching in college. There was girl named, Kavitha, she was a student of mine. She was very brilliant and genius in her studies, but a bit weak in English. At the end of every year, college usually organizes annual day. During this function, the college usually gives away prizes to students who have performed well in all categories, like sports, speeches, studies, etc.. Now, this particular girl who is bit weak in English wished to participate in public speaking competition, but wanted to get first prize and be awarded on the stage. She, somehow, made serious efforts and prepared well for the competition and won the first prize. Here, of course, great efforts were put in and, at the same time, determination and positive thinking played a great role in achieving the desired result.

With that being said, in life, we always face difficult situations, especially in terms of financial crisis and that is the biggest hurdle in life that all of us face and experience. Many people are perplexed whether its good to go with job or with business, some of course do not wish to take risk and continue with the job because it gives security, but the blunt fact is that, we can never get settled down in life with the salary and we can never buy a house or maintain a car. When it comes to business, number of people try different businesses and fail and many approach best astrologers who try to give solutions, but still, some times, they fail to execute them in a proper way. Now, this is the time, they come to conclusion that "its really very difficult to earn money". Here, the main problem is, one must come out of this thought process of difficult to earn money thought. One must strongly believe with great positive thought that we can get what we want.

Believing is still a very small word to consider, for example, I wish for a car after two years, and I believe, I would get it. So, do not think or believe, but think and consider that the wish of car is going to be true after a couple of years and it will done so. We need to keep wishing with positive thoughts that it is going to happen. positive thoughts are like positive signals, energy sparkles or particles that we are showering them into future time and that energy will do miracles for us and we do not have to worry about it at all. We just need to have positive thinking only and have a strong mind that it will happen at any cost and that is called synchronicity. I will discuss about synchronicity in another article with separate heading, called, I am writing my own story.

"Believe in yourself. You are braver than you think, more talented than you know, and capable of more than you imagine." Quotation by Roy T. Bennett. So, in short, have a strong mind and have positive thinking.

<u>Strengthen your aura</u>

Aura is the luminous light and/or energy field that surrounds the human body. The aura has long been described as an electromagnetic energy field that surrounds people like an egg-shaped ball of energy that encompasses the body. First of all, we should be aware that we all of us have aura and we need to see and experience it first. This energy field is sometimes called soul, or spirit. The field contains all of the patterns, karma, traumas, and information from everything that you have ever experienced. You can tell how your energy field is doing by examining how your life is going and how you're feeling about it all. Aura reflects one's own personality, thoughts, emotions, intentions. These energy fields are linked with chakras in our energy field and they are all linked with our personality.

We are basically made of two materials, one is physicality and another one is energy, can be called aura or energy or soul whichever word people use. Our human body is the material body that can touch, feel, and experience so many things. Our universe consists of solar systems, bright stars, asteroids, galaxies, milky way etc....

We, human beings are moving planets on this planet called earth. Everything movement is designed to perform actions in certain pattern and thus, we act accordingly. Astrology delineates exactly our movements in the form of predictions, which is in fact true because it is science. Every human person has a specific pattern about his or her life and lives accordingly. Pattern, I mean, can be habits, emotions, thoughts, tastes, interests, lifestyle, etc.

Now, coming to energy filed like, I mentioned earlier, we have aura encompassing our human body with seven chakras, which function like energy switches. There are basically seven types of chakras in human body and they are,

In Sanskrit, **the Root Chakra** is known as the Mooladhara Chakra; this root defines our relationship with Mother Earth. It influences our passion, creativity, youthfulness, vitality and most importantly, our basic survival instincts. The Root Chakra is represented by the colour red, which is also an indication for the need of logic, realistic thinking and order in our lives.

The Sacral Chakra, or the Swadhisthana Chakra, is symbolic of the water elements present within the human body. It is represented by the colour orange, which tends to impact our ability to be happy and joyful, compassionate, creative and passionate. It also influences our desires, sexuality and our reproductive functions amongst others.

The Solar Plexus Chakra, known as the Manipura Chakra in Sanskrit, is roughly translated to 'City of Jewels' and it is regarded as one of the most powerful chakras that has profound influences on our personal power. The Solar Plexus chakra represents our personal abilities and powers, and it influences both our personal and professional success.

The Heart Chakra, also known as the Anahata Chakra, is associated with the element of air within the body, and it has the most profound influence on our professional and personal relationships.

Vishuddhi Chakra or Throat Chakra symbolises our true inner voice, and our ability to communicate with others. It is represented by the colour blue, and it is associated with our abilities to listen, empathise and communicate with others.

The Brow/Third Eye Chakra, also known as the Ajna Chakra, roughly translates to 'the centre of knowledge or monitoring'. It is symbolised by the colour indigo, and is associated with our sense of thought, our ability to rationalise, use logic and conduct an analysis to reach reasonable conclusions.

The Crown Chakra, known as the Sahasrara Chakra in Sanskrit, is connected with the element of light, and it is associated with several organs and glands within the body, including the brain, the hand, the nervous system and the pituitary gland.

Every life form in the universe emanates a reflection of the energy that composes their being. As higher life forms, humans have the ability to emit light patterns that coincide with personalities, moods, life experiences, and levels of awareness.

Aura colors are contained within the natural forces surrounding the human body. Some people emit low levels of light due to hereditary and environmental factors. Others, have extremely poignant light levels that are easily perceived by people who have the ability to sense and interpret aura thresholds. It's a fact that all living creatures, including humans, emit a radiant spiritual energy that encodes a series of colours. These colours indicate varying degrees of life vitality, mental power, spiritual struggle, and even coinciding factors with time and ethereal elements.

No living being emits only one aura colour, but one colour can be dominant over all others. Every human is imbued with soul, mind, and body powers contributing to a complete aura colour spectrum. Some colours may be nearly non-existent and unperceivable, while other colours permeate an entire aura complex. Extremes in aura colours are not uncommon, but they do indicate a situation of imbalance. Every person should exhibit strains of all aura colors with wider spectral presences of colors that accurately reflect their personalities and mindsets. (https://www.colorpsychology.org/aura-colors/)

Red and pink color aura: These aura colours are intimately intertwined with the physical body. Red light is an indication of strong emotions like anger, love, and pride. It is also the most primal colour signalling the presence of the need to act aggressively, or make a show of personal strength. The deeper the red light, the stronger the primal passion. As red light fades into pink, it signals a weakening of some personal facet that involves both body and spirit. True pink light is a sure indication that a person is feeling vulnerable in some way. This can be negative like having a fear regarding professional performance, or positive like recently being stricken with the possibility of finding true love.

Blue and Indigo color aura: People with very strong blue aura lights are strong and calm individuals. They tend to seek solace in places where other people fail to look. Blue light people are often incredibly intuitive, and lean toward disciplines that involve human interaction. Extremely strong blue aura lights are an indication that a person possesses extraordinary sensory abilities that could include untapped psychic abilities.

Magenta colour aura: Emitting extreme amounts of brilliant magenta aura light coincides with the need to be an eccentric. This colour is very rare as a dominant aura colour, but is very evident in people who constantly have the compulsion to go against the status quo. Magenta is a colour symbolizing struggle, but isn't necessarily negative. It is often an indicator of artistic abilities that have yet to be realized.

Orange colour aura: Brilliant orange auras are the surest indicator of vigour and vitality. This colour is common in people who are athletically competitive and successful in areas of personal performance. This surety can also be formed from sexual prowess and pride. Some people who are on the verge of becoming unhinged in their interaction with others exhibit strong orange auras.

Yellow and Gold colour aura: These colours are very common in people who value the pursuit of cognitive honing and discipline. The closer a yellow aura is to a golden one, the more deeply involved a person is in philosophical matters. Brilliant gold auras are often attached to people who are experiencing difficulties with the concerns of life and personal placement in the universe. People with golden auras often possess a love-hate relationship with time.

Brown and Tan colour aura: Earthy auras indicate personalities that struggle with logical and methodical aspects of life. This struggle can be capped with either cold calculation, or an emotional formula. Tan light people must constantly be aware that they tend to over-think normal conundrums, and can often be perceived by others as uptight and elusive.

Green aura light appears when a person is in a period of healing, or is in a state of extreme good health. This is a colour indicating the perfect balance between bodily health, mental security, personal relationships, and emotional outlooks. People exhibiting a constant dominant green aura light are natural healers.

Violet and Lavender colour aura: The deeper the purple aura light, the closer a person is to achieving spiritual freedom. Extremely sensual people, and those needing constant interpersonal contact exhibit strong purple and lavender light.

White and Crystalline colour aura: Clear and brilliant white light is extremely rare and only present in people who have strongly developed spiritual awareness. This light is mostly found in spiritual leaders like yogis, life counsellors, and other gurus.

Black is commonly misunderstood as a negative aura light. It is never a sure indicator of the presence of undesired spiritual qualities. It does indicate however, that a person is under some sort of veil of protection. This can be due to a physical ailment, or emotions like worry and fear.

Now, having said, I would like to discuss some key elements on how we should protect ourselves from negative forces and increase our aura with positive energy. Some of the key points are as follows,

> ➢ Make conscious effort to make lifestyle changes, keeping your thoughts checked always and do not judge others, criticize or think negative about others.

- Always listen to good music, uplifting music, which is energizing, which creates positive energy.
- Visit places that have positive vibes, you will feel better.
- Read good books.
- Do physical exercises, go to gym, do yoga, etc..
- Use some religious articles like crystals, malas, rudraksha, etc.., which will act as a shield against negative energy.
- Being content with what you have.
- Develop an attitude of gratitude.
- Spend time in water, take shower, etc.. as the water the closest element that is connected to the source (pure light and/or pure energy).
- Practice random acts of kindness, love, compassion, forgiveness, gratitude, help others, charity, etc.. When you forgive others, you are emptying negative force from yourself and inviting positive energy into yourself and you will be at peace.
- Self-realization, introspect yourself, discover yourself.
- Keep yourself vibrated with positive energy by wearing a smile and be happy and laugh, watch videos or movies that generate laughter.
- Always remain calm and patient when dealing with negative people, try to avoid them, and in case, in

unavoidable situations, keep yourself silent, make sure you do not react to any emotional stimulus.

➢ Accept when you are faced with negativity and allow it to subside on its own, it's like when the night comes, the night has to disappear and light will indeed come.

➢ Keep your house illuminated, use rock salt to clean the house, to mop the house.

➢ Always, think in terms of energy, frequency, and vibration and have a strong and clear visualization, and develop good visualization techniques, which will help a great deal.

➢ Have a good companion who can really appreciate you and is positive about you.

➢ Spend time with nature, talk to a tree, beach, etc..

Everything is made of energy and we are energy and that energy is vibrating at a certain frequency and our job is to match that frequency (pattern) of what we want, for example, to get a particular channel in radio, we need to tune the radio properly until we get a particular channel. Likewise, we have what we call, brain waves in our energy field and we need to tune our brainwaves. How we do this is, we need to make conscious effort to speak positive words, have clear visualization and corresponding vibration and feelings. It's like acting, we need to get in that particular role in order to get things done, for example, mannerisms, feelings, emotions of that character. We do we manager this energy, stop haemorrhaging energy, conserve it, keep focussed and accumulate it. Have yourself focussed and have good concentration, do not get distracted. Perhaps, it's better to do small concentration exercises on a daily basis and we can start seeing positive results.

Recharging the body with cosmic energy

On a daily basis, from morning to evening, we are so engaged with our job and/or work and, by the end of the day, we are completely exhausted physically and mentally and we need very good sleep in order to boost our body and mind with fresh energy for the next day. Human body is a special gift to everyone. It is comprised of physical, mental and spiritual nature.

Physical body: The physical body is a bundle of motions, a combination of cells composed of moving molecules, which in turn are made up of whirling atoms, composed of protons, electrons, neutrons, positrons and mesons whirling in the relatively immense space within each atom. These minute, semi-intelligent forms are manifestations of sparks of thought, from the infinite energy. Underlying the chemical motion in the cells are dancing waves of molecular motions, beneath which surge waves of atomic motion. Human body is a miracle. It contains complex organic system and functionality. It needs good food, water, oxygen, proper sunlight and nature.

In order to maintain good physical body and keep oneself in good health, one must follow some rules and regulations in order to keep the physical body in good condition, and they are,

> ➢ Exercise daily and walk small distances minimum.
> ➢ Eat fresh and organic vegetables that are readily available in the market.
> ➢ Have sufficient sleep, lack of sleep can cause symptoms of depression, anger, anxiety, and other physical related illnesses.
> ➢ Spend time in nature
> ➢ Use preventive measures and take care of your body.
> ➢ Eat a variety of healthy foods.
> ➢ Control your meal portions.
> ➢ Stop smoking and protect yourself against second-hand smoke.
> ➢ Drink plenty of liquids and fruit juices rather than alcohol contained products.
> ➢ Adjust and have a balanced form of diet, which includes all nutrients and multivitamins.

Human body sustains not only with material food and drink, but with cosmic energy that flows through us through medulla oblongata, which is located at the base of the brain, where the back of the skull joins the neck. Human body is completely surrounded by this cosmic energy that continually keeps protecting and energizes.

Spiritual body: The spiritual body in simple words mean, energy body, which we cannot see with our physical eyes, but can be experienced. Some of us call it soul, some call it atma (spirit), whichever the term we use for spiritual body, it has no limits like physical body. It can transcend everywhere. It has infinite knowledge about everything. Being in the human body, one needs to communicate with the spirit, in other words, talk with yourself in the silence because spirit does not need language. One just needs to calm down and listen to what your spirit is trying to say to you.

A spiritually well person seeks harmony between what lies within as well as the physicality.

Some of the things that one can achieve in order to retain this balance and they are,

➢ Practice meditation daily.

- ➢ Learn to work with energy (through practices such as Huna, Reiki, chi gong, and acupuncture) as a way to keep the energy channels open.
- ➢ Study consciousness, religion, or philosophy.
- ➢ Attend a silent retreat to deepen your connection to Self.
- ➢ Spend time alone/meditate regularly.
- ➢ Be fully present in everything you do.
- ➢ Allow yourself and those around you the freedom to be who they are.
- ➢ See opportunities for growth in the challenges life brings you

Mental body: On a surface level, the mental body is your thoughts. On a deeper level, it is the domain of your beliefs, desires, values, and goals. Beliefs are opinions and convictions that we hold as being true without having immediate proof. Values represent what we hold internally as most important in an area of life. Values and beliefs can come from thoughts that were formed very early in childhood.

There are always two ways to travel in life one leads to happiness and one leads to sorrow. One should view time and space as they come to you in the form of problems, experiences, and relations.

Emotions play a great role in everyone's life. If they are treated appropriately, one can have a peaceful life, otherwise, these emotions can defeat you and say, see, I have won the battle. They are like soldiers of wrong thoughts rally to attack your inner peace, so, when you encounter these soldiers, then, it is time for you to wake up the soul soldiers of light honesty, self-control, and discipline to wage battle against them.

Stop complaining: One must avoid the company of those who always complain and grumble and in fact, it only creates negative vibrations and does not give inner peace. We should never complain, though it causes great discomfort. If one is able to attack negative force or energy with patience and self-control, then, without any further doubt, you have won the battle of emotions. It is natural for anyone to be swimming in the ocean of emotions, but all these can be achieved gradually and one must put efforts in order to achieve this discipline. For example, lets say, you are or your wife started an argument on a silly issue and she keeps shouting and yelling at you for the wrong decision you have made, so, in this situation, what would be your reaction or if your husband does the same, keeps yelling and shouting at the top of his lungs for no reason at all. The best thing that I would advise is, to keep silent and not talk at all, and perhaps, after some time, she or he will quite down, considering that they have won the battle, but in fact, you have won the battle through self-discipline, which is a positive energy. This practice of fighting the battle is not that easy, it comes only by practice

Hence, in short, be king over yourself, letting the soldiers of goodness and good habits rule the kingdom of your mind, then, happiness will reign within you forever. Fear, anxiety, depression, all these are biggest enemies and one should courageously fight them with love and patience.

Favourite person is my mother

The loving mother, very dear,

With every gift in every prayer,

As a mother who draws us near,

To comfort our every fear.

Mother in thy arms, we rest,

Where peace and happiness exist,

Who takes nothing, but with loving heart,

Procures blessings at any cost.

A mother with her child in hand,

Holds tight to her right hand,

With the shining face on this land,

Stands firm and calm.

She has a tender human heart,

Pierced by a sword and torn apart,

How hard to imagine, oh mother,

The pain with one another.

We forget to think at dawn,

About the lord and his marvellous deeds,

As a mother, she is in every town,

To guard her offspring in every need.

The efficacy of the rosary

the rosary has mysteries,

with unexplained history,

merged with love and compassion,

it is our mother's guide to salvation.

The relation strengthens with garland by Mary,

To the family who has Mary of Rosary,

Darkness overshadows when we turn away,

From the love of Rosary in life, we may lack.

The day shines like a diamond in the sky,

The stars appear after the long day,

Night and day make no difference,

To the rosary who stands firm with continence.

My heart burns like the fire,

With woes like broken tyres,

How hard to face dilemma and strife,

With a lovable gift in my life.

Joy inexpressible I shall meet,

WIth the discovery of Rosary when I get,

The Rosary and I with astounding joy,

My heart fills with love in a day.

Sleep paralysis in dreams

Sleep is an important element of human life. Human body is a complex machine unlike any other machine that requires rest for certain period of time. Sleep is a naturally recurring state of mind and body, characterized by altered consciousness, relatively inhibited sensory activity, reduced muscle activity and inhibition of nearly all voluntary muscles during rapid eye movement sleep, and reduced interactions with surroundings.

Human body does indeed need a few hours and/or sufficient hours of sleep and it needs to be switched off completely before it gets rejuvenated, activated and energized for the body to get into action and to continue with daily activities. Unlike food and drink, sleep gives lot of energy and boost to human body, that is why it is very much essential that we sleep and/or have a sound sleep during the night.

During sleep, our body is completely relaxed, but human brain is at work. Here, the biggest question that can arise to anyone, that is, what if one is disturbed during this sound sleep with nightmares or other disturbing dreams. If one experiences these things, one experiences tiredness, exhaustion, depression, anxiety, etc. Sleep does indeed acts as a powerful pill to forget worries, depression, concerns, etc. It works to give pleasant dreams and/or to get good rest if the body is not feeling well. Sleep is not an escape for problems because once one wakes up the next morning, the same issue would continue. Hence, those issues must be sorted out in order to get good sleep.

Sleep paralysis is the word or term that one might have come across in life, sometime or the other. People who have gone through this kind of experience will know what it means by sleep paralysis. This is the state of mind where the human body experiences terrifying nightmares and the body becomes paralyzed for a few minutes and one cannot actually come out of that state, however one tries to. The main reason is due to an irregularity in passing between the stages of sleep and wakefulness.

Various causes can be identified as the root of sleep paralysis, but however, there could be many other factors that can possibly contribute to sleep paralysis. Some of the contributing factors are, as per my experience,

- Lack of sleep.
- Stress and depression.
- Lack of love and affection from parents or from others since childhood.
- Mental conditions like emotional disturbances, imbalance in thinking, wrong breathing, etc.
- Wrong sleeping positions, its advised that one must sleep on the right hand side and not on the left hand side as it puts pressure on the heart and as a result, it causes disturbance in sleep patterns.

Sleep paralysis consists of experiences of hallucinations of aliens, ghosts, electricity passing through the body, hearing strange voices, etc... Researchers have discovered that two brain chemicals such as glycine and gaba are responsible for this sort of muscle paralysis. During these episodes, people cannot really move or speak anything until that phase is completed. These sort of episodes pass on and will be concluded with a few minutes, but the person going through these kind of experiences feels that for hours. Some people have reported these experiences and felt that they were going to die because these are unnatural occurrences and are unthinkable. These episodes usually occurs during two transitions and they are,

➤ Between falling asleep.

➤ Waking up.

It can usually happen when one's body is having trouble making this transition and/or perhaps, there could be various other factors that could be involved or contributing to these episodes of sleep paralysis.

Lasya with sleep paralysis: I am trying to narrate in the first person because its quite feasible to narrate the story and/or experiences.

I am sleeping, I see some dark figures, some kind of moving bodies, but they are very dark in nature. I was sleeping on the bed. I could see it and I knew it was a dream, but I could not move. My body trembled. These figures slowly climbed on bed and sat on my stomach and after some time, three of them enter into my stomach as if there was an entrance or a door through which they could enter. Once they disappeared through my stomach, I woke up with terror and gasping for breath and could not sleep for hours.

During another time of the night, I still wonder why these things happen during the night as if these creatures are afraid to face us during the day. So, the other day, perhaps, few years back, I still can remember that I was too tired and wanted to go to sleep immediately. So, as I lay down on bed, just thought about God and slowly and slowly and gradually slipped into the world of dreams. I was not aware of my surroundings until a few minutes, perhaps and forgot the sensation of my body, but all of sudden, I suddenly began experiencing electricity passing through my stomach, which was quite puzzling. Initially, I thought, it could be due to some other reasons, so, I decided to wake up immediately and get the issue solved, but to my surprise, I could not move my body. I was trying to speak and shout in terror, but words could not come out of my mouth. It was like physiotherapy treatment where they usually treat patients who experience muscle pains or contractions. It was like flow of electricity, not continuously, but like electricity passes and gives a break for a fraction of second and then flows again and this experience lasted for a few minutes, and at the same time, I heard some strange voices, which were really threatening. Once I came out of this phase, I got out of my bed, had a sip of water and could not sleep a few hours again.

These kinds of experiences I had, lasted for many years and I had no clue as to why it has been happening to me. On another day, it was during the day, it was roughly about 8 in the morning. I was still feeling sleepy, so, went to sleep again, but I had a clear dream, much clearer than the real life. I could not really make out if this was true or dream. During this episode, I was walking towards my room, walked into my room and slept and covered the bedsheet fully and I could sense that some one was walking up and down my body as if they were trying to wake me up. At this time, I did get bit scared, but when I woke up, I was searching for real answers to these occurrences, but could not find one until today.

So, today, sleep paralysis is a very common occurrence and we have easy access to internet and other available resources to search for in order to find solutions. In short, there is nothing to be afraid of sleep paralysis and this is very common thing.

<u>In search of heavenly diamonds</u>

We, as human beings are living on this planet earth. It is always a puzzling thing how life exits on this planet that keeps rotating around itself and around the sun. There seems to be a complexity of confusion when anyone tries to explore the space because with physical eyes, we cannot find anything except vastness of space with different planets, solar systems, galaxies etc... So, always, we must question ourselves as to who we are and what are we. If we try to look at the world and try to get answers with physical eyes, there is always a limitation and we cannot go beyond a certain point because there is a world beyond these physical eyes and what we see is not a real world. There is much, much brighter, larger, clearer world that is present beyond our physical body. This physicality is only a limitation.

Once, multitude of angels has gathered around in heaven in the presence of GOD. GOD wanted to test them and gave them a test. He told them, "go to any planet that you find in this cosmos and get me a beautiful gift". So, angels were divided into different teams and spread themselves out and went ahead with their travel to different planets of this cosmos in search of something that could be given a best gift to GOD.

One set of angels came to the planet called, Nirupuza, which is almost 5 million light years from the planet Earth. To describe briefly about this planet, Nirupuza, it's a beautiful planet. Natural resources of this planet are bit different than Earth. On planet Nirupuza, they have everything similar to planet Earth, like trees, water, animals, different forms of life unlike human beings, but their appearance is somewhat different and they do not speak, but they communicate through thoughts, and what we call telepathy. Trees on this planet basically shine like light and leaves have multitude of colors, let's say for example, if the leave is in blue color, it shines and glows like radium object even during the day and during the night also. Likewise, some trees have different colors and their leaves with some other colors, but they all shine and glow like radium objects. Now, when it comes to water, density of water is very thin, so thin like air and wind on planet Earth, but water is visible to human eyes like diamonds and water shines like light and it flows in the form of rivers and oceans. One can swim in the water if one wishes and one can float also. They can also breathe in the water and there is no chance of anyone drowning in the water and die. Now, when it comes to their physical bodies, they are so light like eagles and they have wings and they can fly if wish to in order to travel from one place to another. They have beautiful mountains with so much of plantation. The most amazing thing is with animals on this planet. These animals do not hurt anyone because all are vegetarians only and wonderful thing is these animals speak our human language, but they have different words and meanings, which we cannot understand. The physical structure of human like figures are so beautiful beings.

Now, having said that, these angels went to this planet, saw that everything, was so beautiful and searched everywhere. These angels almost spent about a month in search of a beautiful thing and/or object. As they kept searching for days and months, they came near to waterfalls. It was amazing falls and cannot really describe in words, so, angels thought that this could be the amazing gift that they could gift to GOD. So, they have taken this water falls from there and went to heaven.

Next set of angels went to another planet, called Gracflid. Here, the life of the planet is completely different and perhaps, located 2 billion light years from Earth. Here, beings are of different nature and they have different kind of language through which they communicate with each other. These beings do not really walk on the ground, they always keep flying in the air. They have ability to produce anything they wish at any time. Suppose, they are in need of food or house or anything, they will just clap their hands or fingers, and then, immediately, things will appear to them like a magic. Animal like creatures are also present, but they are very huge in size, but they are harmless. They have horses, so beautiful and they have wings and they can fly anywhere they wish. So, these angels also searched different places on this planet and were unable to find most beautiful thing, but after a long search, they found one beautiful horse, a flying horse. They thought, GOD definitely will love this horse since its multi-coloured and it has wings and can fly anywhere. Hence, they have taken that flying horse and went to heaven.

Next, another batch of angels have come to planet Earth, now, on this planet, these angels found it extremely difficult to find anything beautiful. It is mainly because they have come from heaven and they are not able to find any objects better than heaven. Now, having searched everywhere tirelessly and spoke to themselves, that they have wasted their energy by having come to this planet as they are unable to find any good objects as gifts. Now, without much disappointment, after having searched for years, they decided to go back to heaven without any gift, but at last, as they were leaving this planet, they witnessed a couple of incidents on this planet, one is, lovers making love and another one is mother is bathing one year kid and the kid is so happy, smiling and laughing so loudly because the kid is experiencing happiness in the hands of his mother. So, angels decided to wait for a moment and continued to watch very closely the scene of month and kid. They felt a bit amazing at this scene. So, they have taken this and went to heaven as a gift.

Now, almost, all batches of angles were present in the presence of GOD. Everyone was waiting and looked at each other's gifts and felt amazed about each other's gifts, but most of the angels felt amused about the gift of mother and kid and considered it as a funny. Now, GOD has arrived and everyone presented their gifts to GOD. He saw them and appreciated them for their wonderful efforts. He came across the gift of mother and kid and felt overwhelmed and said, this is the best gift that I have ever seen. Everyone was surprised at this, but did not understand why GOD liked this mother and kid gift so much. GOD then said, "you have brought me the things that I have created and they are indeed so beautiful, but these angels brought me mother and kid, and this exhibits the greatness and love mother has for her son. I am GOD and GOD means love. So, they brought love for me and I am love and they gifted me ME (love)."

How to be meek and humble

Analyze your thoughts and see on what throne of consciousness your ego is seated, what kind of consciousness is predominant in your mind. Try to be humble instead of egotistical and through magnetism of humbleness, can attract the protecting presence of friends, strangers, and so on. Humbleness is a fertile valley of consciousness where the rain of God's wisdom falls fruitfully. As on a mountain peak no rain can gather, so also on an upthrust ego, no waters of knowledge can collect. Egotism shuts the door of recipience through which knowledge enters. Humbleness opens the portals wide and bids all wisdom come within. Egotism is an obvious ugliness written on the face of the egotist and repels people, whereas humbleness is a fragrance that makes the bearer sweetly attractive to all. Humbleness is born of wisdom or knowledge of one's true self.

Egotism: It refuses to investigate the truth. It slaps wisdom in the face. It reveals its smallness by ineffectually trying to make others feel small. It is the brittle imitation armor of deluded souls. It repels friends and truth. The egotist is a like an empty vessel, makes much noise. The man with egotism has plenty of time to speak to others of his importance because he is not busy performing outstanding deeds. As a result of all these, he does not progress into a good person.

You will reap what you sow: If you want to be loved, start loving others who need your love. If you expect others to be honest with you, then, start being honest with yourself. If you do not want others to be wicked, then you must avoid doing evil to yourself. If you want others to sympathize with you, start showing sympathy to those around you. If you want to be respected, you must learn to be respectful to everyone, both young and old. If you want a display of peace from others, you must be establish peace with yourself. If you want others to be religious, start becoming spiritual yourself first. Suppose, if you happen to visit a valley or a forest where there is complete silence, you should with loud voice and the words will come back to you. It is like boomerang, if you throw it and it will bounce back to you.

Law of service: The law of service to others is secondary and corollary to the law of self-interest or self-preservation, which may be termed selfishness. No sane man ever does anything without a reason. No action is performed without reference to a direct or indirect thought, which is selfish. Giving service is indispensable to receiving service; therefore, to serve others by giving financial, mental, or moral help is to find self-satisfaction. You can prove that service is not wholly unselfish by asking yourself this question, if you knew beyond a doubt that by service to others, your own soul would be lost rather than strengthened, would you serve.

Resurrect your consciousness: One important thing you have to do is resurrect your consciousness from the environment of ignorance. You must blame yourself for environmental troubles, which you have been creating, consciously or unconsciously somewhere sometime in the past. Free yourself from all neuroses or complexes. You are neither man nor a woman. You are not what you think you are, you are an energy, immortal. Meditation, exercise, relaxation, self-control, right diet, fortitude, and positive attitude of the mind is very essential to everyone. Your traits may be good, but your greatest enemy is your ego.

Ego's failure: Man's attachment to matter keeps the soul confined to the body prison and prevents it from finding freedom, the Source, the realm of eternal bliss. The ego attempts to satisfy through material channels the soul's constant longing for GOD. The soul's hunger can never be appeased by indulging the senses. When man realizes this and masters his ego, then, he achieves self-control and life will become glorified and he will find meaning in life.

An inferiority complex is born of a secret awareness of real or imagined weaknesses. In trying to compensate for such weaknesses, a person may build an armor of false pride and exhibit an inflated ego. Then, those who do not understand the real cause of such an attitude may say the person has a superiority complex.

Elements of spiritual eye

In order to behold the kingdoms of astral phenomena, the Christ pervaded cosmos and eternity beyond, the human soul has to withdraw the matter-circumscribed vision of the two physical eyes and penetrate it through the telescopes of the astral eye, the Christ and the cosmic eye. The physical eyes can see only a little segment of the whole world, but when the vision of the two mundane eyes is made single and the consciousness penetrates through the start in the opal-blue astral eye, as represented by the little white star just above the human eyes, then the vision is enlarged and the devotee beholds his astral body and other astral visions. In order to understand this concept, I would illustrate with an example. On rishi or saint, sitting on the banks of the Ganga. He was thinking of something mundane when his mind spontaneously started going from under him and the sky was expanding and receding. A moment later, he experienced a terrible force springing up from the base of his body like an atomic explosion. He felt that he was vibrating very fast, the light currents were terrific. He experienced the supreme bliss, like the climax of the man's desire and it continued for a long time. His while body was contracting until the feeling of pleasure became quite unbearable and he completely lost awareness of his body.

While taking baptism with John, Jesus saw the spiritual eye as a starry dove descending from heaven when his guru, John the Baptist baptized him. Your spiritual guru helps you to open your spiritual eye. The little star in the center symbolizes the mouth of the dove and its wings are a blue and a golden light. The spiritual eye consists of a white start palpitating in the heart of an opal-blue light surrounded by a golden ring. The spiritual eye is the epitome of the Holy Spirit. The gold ring represents cosmic energy, the blue, Christ consciousness. Piercing the blue tunnel one can enter into the white start tunnels in the Christ eye and the cosmic eye, by whose rays the devotee penetrates the walls of matter to reach the Source, the unmanifested kingdom of pure ever new blessedness of spirit and energy. This physical body of ours Is a physical wall between that spirit world and physical world.

Power in the spiritual eye: One cannot enter the star in the spiritual eye until, by practice of Kriya. One is able to become breathless, and to withdraw all energy and concentration from the five telephones of the senses. A spiritual eye is also called Kundalini and it is conceived of as the primal power or energy. In terms of modern psychology, it can be called the unconscious in man. In Hindu mythology, it represents to the concept of kali. In the philosophy of Shaivism, the concept of kundalini is represented by the shivalingam, the oval shaped stone or pillar with a snake coiled around it. However, most commonly, kundalini is illustrated as a sleeping serpent coiled three and a half times. Of course, there is no serpent residing in mooladhara, sahasraa or any other chakra, but the serpent has always been a symbol for efficient consciousness. In all the mystic cults of the world, you will find the serpent and if you have seen any pictures or images of Lord Shiva, you will have noticed serpents girdling his waist, neck and arms. Kali is also adorned with serpents and Lord Vishnu eternally reposes on a large coiled serpent; this serpent power symbolizes the unconscious in man. This unconscious is the doorway to energy world.

Spiritual eye Awakening: In the traditional descriptions of kundalini awakening, it is said that kundalini resides in mooladhara in the form of a coiled snake and when the snake awakens, it uncoils and shoots up through sushumna, the psychic passage in the center of the spirinal cord, opening the other chakras as it goes.Brahmachari swami describes the awakeing as, "Sadhakas have seen the sushumna in the form of a luminous rod or pillar, a golden yellow snake or sometimes as a shining black snake about ten inches long with blood red eyes like smoldering charcoal, the front part of the tongue vibrating and shining like lightening ascending the spinal column."

The meaning of the three coils of the serpent is as follows, the three coils represent the three mantras of om, which relate to past, present and future, to the gunas, tamas, rajas and sattwa, to the three states of consciousness, waking, sleeping and dreaming and to the three types of experience, subjective experience, sensual experience, and absence of experience. The half coil represents the state of transcendence, where there is neither waking, sleeping nor dreaming, so, the three and half signlfy the total experience of the universe and the experience of the transcendence.

Everyone can and has to kundalini. With the awakening, visions of GOD take place and awakening of supernatural faculties. Kundalini is the creative energy. It is the energy of creative force and self expressions. It is reproduction of new life. It is the same energy when someone composes or plays beautiful music. It is the same energy, which is expressed in all parts of life, whether it is building up a business, fulfilling the family duties or reaching whatever goal you aspire for. These are all expressions of the same creative energy.

Divine Birthright: Everybody, whether householder or rishis or saints, that the awakening of kundalini is the prime purpose of human incarnation. All the pleasures of sensual life, which we are enjoying now are intended only to enhance the awakening of kundalini amidst the adverse circumstances of human life. When kundalini awakens, physical body actually undergoes many changes, generally, they are positive. You must change your status from that of a mortal beggar to that of a divine son. Instead of supplicating, you must demand what belongs to you by right as a divine child. As a human being, it is your birthright to access to divinity, no matter what you are and in what state you are in. By means of kundalini awakening, you are compensating for the laws of nature and speeding up the pace of your physical, mental and spiritual evolution. Once awakened, every cell is charged with the high voltage prana of kundalini and when the total awakening occurs, man becomes a junior GOD, an embodiment of divinity.

<u>Never say, YES, to self-pity from others</u>

We hear so many people saying, ayyoopapam, poor thing, feeling upset, so sad and so on. These are words that can be soothing and consoling, but in fact, they are unnecessary sympathy and displaying pity, which is negative energy.It is an exaggerated sense of pity over one's own life, position or circumstance.

"Self-pity is our worst enemy and if we yield to it, we can never do anything wise in this world."- Helen Keller

If you think, you are placed in a lower rank or lower stratum of the society and you do not have any proper resources, do not feel bad or get disappointed. Be brave, do not accept to show pity on you, that is very bad. Suppose, one of your family members not feeling well and unable to eat good food, that person should not feel bad that others are able to eat good food and never accept pity or feel self-pity, which is negative energy.

Craving for drama: Many people try to create the scene and make the scene of their problems or success, because they want to create an identity in the society or family or in any organizations, like a drama queen. These kinds of people make fuss of everything. When this kind of drama happens, lot of attention is given to the situation that has just happened and people who have witnessed the scene will talk about it, both negatively and positively and this in fact creates kind of consolation to the person who has created the scene. It is like seeking identity in the public.

Past-oriented person: No matter whatever the past, you must not think about it and must throw the past and preserve it in the library of the mind. You must consider it as an experience that was meant for you to go through in life. Consider it as a blessing and not as a curse. Many of us in life, would have gone through many difficult situations and it does not mean, only I had very rough situations, very tough life since ages and nothing good seems to be happening. You must try and avoid these negative images and thoughts of the past and do not remain in the past because past is past and it is gone and no long present, so why should we bother about past.

Low self-esteem: Suppose, lets say, we are gifted with some precious gift, either gold, silver, diamond or anything, we preserve it and wear it whenever we like to wear it. We give so much value to that gift. In the same way, our human body is the greatest gift that is give to us and so, why should we insult this body by feeling so low. It is the most expensive and priceless gift and cannot be priced. So, whatever the qualities you have, never compare with others and feel low that you are no better or have less skills than others. Never, ever think that you are no good because no one has the right to judge anyone and feel low spirited just because you do not possess qualities that others have. Low self-esteem is a negative energy and should be avoided.

"Confront the dark parts of yourself, and work to banish them with illumination and forgiveness. Your willingness to wrestle with your demons will cause your angels to sing." - August Wilson

Melancholic temperament: These kinds of people are considered to be introverted, analytical, logical and private. When it comes to emotions and feelings, since they do not communicate much with others, they tend to store their emotions within themselves and this is called bottling up of emotions. This is the reason why, emotional balance is not stable for these kinds of people and they tend to blast out whenever small emotional trigger occurs.

Brooding: There is a tendency of developing brooding mind with these kinds of people. It is very dangerous. As human beings, we all make mistakes and errors in life and none of us are perfectionists. It leads to depression, which is another psychological disorder. It does not help and in fact, creates negative energy and one cannot be peaceful when people experience anxiety and depression. Brooding, in other words is thinking on something over and over again with unnecessary thoughts.Brooding is highly toxic. Brooders see their own problems as debilitating and sabotages any real effort to make things better. It leads to all sorts of negative feelings.

Craving for sympathy: Suppose, let us say, one student in a particular college is doing some degree. He or she is very sensitive. Everyone is studying well except him, and he feels let down because of his low scores. Everyone in the college see him as a dull guy and whenever someone sees him, they tell him, "poor guy" and for these kinds of expressions, he feels satisfied because he is getting some sort of sympathy. We should never crave for sympathy and instead work hard on weaknesses. There is a principle that is called, "never accept failure if you have failed so many times" and develop positive attitude. Perhaps, with positive mind, one should be able to say, in spite of many failures and attempts to succeed in something, I have not failed, each time, I failed as you say, I have learned something new and I have gained experience and learnt many new things in life and this is called being positive.

Mental toughness:

- Recognize warning signs of unnecessary emotions.
- Channelize negative thoughts into productive behavior and into productivity.
- Practice gratitude.
- Appreciate yourself and help others.
- Refuse to complain and never use negative words and only about positiveness of others because everyone has some element of positiveness and negativity.
- Never accept that you have failed and never give up.
- Positive attitude.
- Be strong and be tough and build mental strength, especially in times of problems and troubles.

- ➢ Try to be extrovert and communicate with others.
- ➢ Never allow yourself to be taken advantage of because you are very special and you need to be respected.

The Expected inflation rate in India 2035

Inflation is a quantitative measure of the rate at which the average price level of a basket of selected goods and services in an economy increases over a period of time. It indicates a decrease in the purchasing power of a nation's currency, which means, today's 10 rupees will become tomorrow 20 rupees. A few years back, when we received salary of 5000 rupees, it was a great amount because that 5000 rupees had great power to purchase so many things and a family can survive on that amount and in fact, consider savings also, but the same family needs 50,000 rupees in order to get that same thought process. Inflation is when you pay 100 rupees for the ten rupee haircut you used to get.

Causes: Demand and supply are the main reason behind this inflation. When people start consuming more goods and services, this usually occurs in the general scenario. Lets talk in the form of example, suppose, there is a tomato seller in the market who sells tomatoes on a daily basis and he has been doing that since ten years. In a general scenario, when does the tomato prices soar up, its usually when the supply is less. For example, lets say, tomato price is 20 rupees today and supply is good in the market, then, price will remain the same until and unless the seller decides to increase the price depending on the customers. In certain circumstances, it can happen that he has sold all the tomatoes and only 2 kilos of tomatoes are remaining and now, there are about 5 people asking for the same tomatoes and no more tomatoes remaining in the market, the seller will likely increase the price to even 50 or 100 rupees, that is because the supply for that day is very less. People whoever can afford to pay that extra bucks of rupees will pay and buy it. So, in general scenario, not only vegetables, but prices of all goods and things will keep fluctuating depending on its supply.

New generation: Basically speaking, every year, an employee gets increment that is only to meet the expenses of the cost of living. Practically speaking, there is no increment at all because getting increment is only kind of balancing with the cost of living and a slight increase in the power of purchase of goods and things. Suppose, any banks sanctions loans to people, then, in that situation, there is likelihood of high prices. A decade back, when the software was blooming, especially in South India and cities like Bangalore and Hyderabad, software professional were getting good salaries, and many government employees also got tempted, left their present jobs in order to get software jobs. It was at this time, many shopping malls and inox cinemas concept came into being. Many knew, standards of living needed to be increased because there were many people with good salaries and who could afford to buy things at any cost and at any price. Many industries, especially software industry had 5 days of work in a week and they used to spend weekends in these malls and at cinemas. Banks used to rush to them to offer them huge loans because of their attractive salaries. The situation and circumstances are the same, even today also. Big salaries means, big purchases and expensive purchases and we are not going anywhere. The reason being, at one time, we could and were able to purchase a decent house in a few lakhs, but today, because of this high inflation, prices have doubled and tripled up and soaring and skyrocketing the sky.

Buying power in the coming days: Time value of money teaches the principle that money today has reduced purchasing power in the future due to inflation, but increased purchasing power due to investment return.A figure that appears big today may not be sufficient to take care of all your future financial needs. This is important because the value of money does not stay same forever.

There are many companies and banks today, asking and luring us to invest into something, perhaps better than fixed deposits, which in fact, highly luring, but they are useless. For example, if I invest one lakh rupees every year up to ten years, the company promises to give 20 plus lakhs in return, but if we seriously calculate, its not that much worth because if the plan is really good, then, in that case, they must be willing to pay at least 40 to 50 lakhs of lump sum amount after 15 to 20 years, or else, it is loss to our capital amount that we invested for over these 10 years.

(https://www.upwardly.in/blog/is-1-crore-enough-after-15-years-for-all-your-needs/)

For example, to find how much is Rs. 1 crore in 15 years use the division factor of 2.8. That means, Rs 1 crore today will be worth (1 crore/2.8) approximately Rs. 36 lakhs after 15 years.

The greatest enemy, is ignorance

Earning money and investing money into something is very much essential these days in order to survive the cost of living. On a daily basis, rupee keeps changing and it is never the same, for example, today's rupee becomes 95 paisa tomorrow. In other words, because of inflation and time, the value of rupee keeps changing day by day. For example, one person has 10 lakhs in his bank account and he has kept the money in his savings account without doing any investment or booking fixed deposit, so, what will happen in this situation. Generally speaking, the bank will provide some minimum interest in order to keep the rupee value ticking, and moreover, after 5 years, the value of 10 lakhs will be decreased to 9 plus lakhs only, though the figure of 10 lakhs will be there, its value will go down. Let me give another example, suppose, I plan to purchase piece of land or plot, let's say, 100 square feet of land for 10 lakhs, which his gettable today, and after 5 years, the value of the same piece of land will be changed and the value might change to 15 lakhs. In other words, if I have to buy the same piece of land after 5 years, I need to borrow another 5 lakhs rupees in order to own that land. So, during this time process, the value of money has decreased. So, in order to face these difficulties, we need to keep doing something with the money, otherwise, the value of money will be lost and we will be at loss.

Share market: We might have come across the word, "share market". It is a nightmare for many, because it is a like black hole that keeps swallowing everything that one has. I would say, share market or stock market is good and bad, because like every streams, it has negative side and positive side. There are many people who are into the stock market and earning lot of money in minutes and hours and some people in days without much effort, but there are so many things that need to be considered in order to reach to that level. Let's take an example of cricket game, it's a game of bat and ball. By watching the match on television, one can think, oh, it's so easy to hit the ball with the bat, but when you really go to the ground and hold the bat properly, oh, here is another thing, first of all, one needs to learn to handle the bat properly and learn to position oneself near the stumps. This process takes a bit of time and then, one must learn to judge the speed of the ball and the techniques of playing with the ball and so on, and likewise, there are so many things to be considered to play the game. Likewise, stock market also has so many techniques and rules and regulations. One needs to understand how the stock market functions and works on a daily basis and how it responds to the daily changing economic growth.

Investment: One might ask a question, can we consider stock market as an investment option. Well, indeed, yes and no, and of course, this answer sounds contradictory. It is like a game of cricket and if you know how to play the game, then only, you can survive and will be able to play the game well and same thing applies here, if you do not have the knowledge of how stocks move and how market functions, one should never think of stock market in terms of investing or getting money from it. According to Clive Granger, "the stock market is like a small row boat on a rough sea, bouncing around as it drifts, whereas the macro economy is like a large ocean liner, very ponderous and difficult to maneuver, but without such a rough journey."

There are multiple investment options that are available for every person and one must think and study, which is best one and which suits good for every person and go accordingly. One cannot blindly go ahead and invest into something, which he or she does not know anything about it. Here, I wish to quote an example, years back, one agent was working for a particular company. I do not wish to mention the name of that company due to personal reasons. Usually speaking, there is bonus and incentives for every agent in every company who works very hard and gets more people into that particular company in the form of insurance of investment. The company is very clear about its terms and plans, but in between, these agents misguide people and make people buy unnecessary policies and convince them to do investments.

Now, this particular agent, convinced nearly certain number of people and made them buy the policy that he wanted and by doing this, he received a gift of car from the company. People who purchased this policy were not aware of the policy terms and conditions, and in fact, they were given wrong information. The policy was market based policy, but people thought that they could get fixed amount of money. Likewise, people can be misguided and agents use people and make them buy lot of policies for their benefits and incentives. In other words, they communicate wrong information and make them believe, that this is the truth.

Good Decision: In today's world, there are many people who are ready to cheat on one another. Here, the problem is not about the fraudsters. There are many fraudsters in the society today who speak sweet words and act like good friends and are so caring. It is ignorance and lack of knowledge and inability to question things that puts people in jeopardy. Here, I wish to give another example, one person, by name, Renuka, she has best friend, who in fact is not a friend at all, she is a wolf in the form of sheep, which Renuka is not aware of it because of her innocence and ignorance. Their friendship lasted for about one year approximately. As Renuka does not have any good friends, she trusted this particular friend and used to share all her personal issues also. Whenever she goes out, she used to go out with her friend, but Renuka used to spend all the money and cover her expenses.

Once, Renuka's friend, swathi asked Renuka her debit card, and Renuka trusted swathi so much and she gave her debit and credit card to her, thinking, she might be in need of some money. Swathi then, used up all the money from the debit card and credit cards and changed her mobile number and never was seen again. Renuka released that she has been cheated, felt helpless. It is always said that, even gold needs to tested in order to prove that this is gold, likewise, its very important to understand, that one must not trust one's shadow these days. One can easily, can come to know others by their behaviour, words and actions. There are so many frauds in society who keep cheating like Swathi (Swathi is fictional name that I have taken).

<u>Kidney stone treatment at home</u>

A person experiences excruciating pain when he or she gets kidney stones. This pain is very hard to describe because it's unbearable. One cannot sit or stand or lay down on bed. In other words, one cannot take any position or posture that gives him comfort and cannot escape from the terrible pain. Kidney stones are basically crystallized objects, very soft in nature and formed in urinary tract or in the kidneys. These stones are never formed in rounded shape and they look like crystallized stones and if they are removed or flushed out of the body, they are like soft mud, can be crushed very easily with fingertips. These such tiny objects, in other words foreign objects create hell to the physical body because human body does not accept any foreign elements or objects entering into physical body or being formed in the body. It immediately reacts through the channel of pain, which is excruciating.

Kidney stones: Kidney stones are hard deposits of minerals and acid salts that stick together in concentrated urine. One experiences lot of pain while passing out of the body. One cannot be guaranteed that one gets only one kidney stone. Kidney stone or kidney stones can be formed in any quantity that is the reason why, it is very essential that one must have sufficient intake of liquids on a daily basis.

One must be wondering as to why these stones get formed within the kidneys. Human body is a complex machine. On a daily basis, human body ingests and/or consumes some quantity of food and liquids. The machine and/or human body is at work and starts the process of digestion, then, the food is broken into small particles and into bits and pieces into almost liquid form. It then transfers to different organs and next, some of the solid mass is converted into energy, some into blood and so on. The remaining food material, which is not necessary or needed for the body is then considered waste and thus, is thrown out of the body in the form of liquidation or feces. This is basically the function of human body and during this process, one must take care to drink plenty of liquids or at least sufficient liquids in order for the flushing system of waste material to get out of the body. If one does not maintain good hydration levels, there is likelihood that some of the waste material would produce unnecessary minerals and get formed into solid deposits and these are called stones, and as a result of this, one experiences severe pain, mainly in the flank and stomach regions. Stone formation is like, for example, one wishes to drink Horlicks or chocolate drink, then, he or she takes a hot cup of milk and mixes coco powder and if he fails to mix the powder well, then, that powder turns into small stone deposits and will remain in the milk. In other words, the chocolate drink is not prepared well. Hence, its not a good drink to have. In the same way, one should not give scope for the mineral deposits to be formed and thus, one can save himself from these kidney stones.

Expensive treatment: Kidney stone/s is not a serious or clinical issue that cannot be treated. Since the evolution of technology and advances in medicine, we have so much medicine available today for every single disease. Today, so much research is taking place in order to treat every grave and small illness that a person is experiencing. These days, usually, whenever a person experiences, he or she usually gets panic and immediately approaches a clinician, which is of course a good thought. Here, the point is, whenever anyone detects or unable to detect or gets diagnosed at the hospital with kidney stones, one should never get worried about it because, it is not a serious issue at all in spite of the fact that it creates and generates very severe pain and would cause anxiety and lead into depression. The clinicians usually suggest surgery to be operated for kidney stones, which is of course, very easy and invasive approach. It is always advisable to try conservative method, give it a time and have patience, and things can get better, and if this does not work, then, one can opt for invasive method of treatment.

Natural remedies and treatment: In order to flush out kidney stones, there is a very simple trick one must follow and dissolving stone is not a big deal at all these days. It all depends on the size of the stone, and depending on that, things can move on a faster pace.

I would suggest a simple technique, which I personally followed and it indeed works well. Once diagnosed for certain that is a kidney stone or stones, as per the instructions or prescription of the physician, pick up the medicines from the drug store, take the dissolving liquids and pain killers, which is very much essential to take whenever one experiences severe pain. Now, here is the thing, get lemon from the market and on a daily basis, squeeze lemon and drink at least one small tea cup of raw lemon early in the morning. I know, the raw lemon does indeed taste bitter, but of course it is very much essential that one must drink this liquid every day in the morning hours as soon as you wake up because this acts as a citric acid and it helps in breaking the stones to small pieces. Then, later one during the day, have yourself hydrated with plenty of butter milk, diluted lemon water, coconut water and plenty of other think liquids. Follow this menu daily. Have a tough thought that the stone will break and come out of your body soon. Whenever you experience severe pain, have yourself medicated with pain killers. I can promise that within one week to ten days, the stones will get melted and will be dissolved through urine. Sometimes, if the stones are very small, one cannot really know or identify that the stone has passed and sometimes, one can easily make out while the stone is being passed and during this time, one must drink plenty of liquids and hold the urine until the bladder is full and then, release the urine. With this small method, the stone will be flushed out very easily. Please remember, since it's a conservative method, make sure that you remain tough in your mind, be strong and confident that things will be better for you, health wise.

Importance of eating at the right time

Food is a like fuel that is essential for human body because it is like a machine that needs to refuel every day. For example, car or bike or any vehicle does not run smoothly or does not run at all if fuel is not filled in time, or just says, it's my vehicle it will listen to me. No way, it will never listen to you unless you fill in sufficient fuel in it, then, that vehicle is very happy. In the same way, human body is a machine that needs fuel or food in time, otherwise, there are tendencies that body can get tired feeling, exhausted, becomes dull, develop headaches, etc.

Importance of food: Eating correct type of food is very important. Food that consists of all nutrients, vitamins, etc.., which should help enriches body and keep the body in good condition. Human body needs certain amount of exercise or walking for the food to get digested properly. A healthy diet always prevents from becoming sick very often because if one does not maintain good balanced diet, it can lead to malnutrition, obesity, chronic illness of unknown cause, heart disease, etc. I wish to give an example here. One person, whom I know personally, he lives very sedentary lifestyle. So, basically, he is a very stout person. So, in order to reduce his weight and pull down some of his weight, he skipped some of his regular meals and he has done this for a month. He has not even been doing any exercises either. Then, after a month or so, he was bedridden for the next three months and had to spend handsome amount of money to get his condition treated. Moreover, apart from the money being spent, he had to experience the pain of illness, which is quite painful. The point of being ill and going through the experience of being ill and suffering the illness is something unthinkable for anyone and no one wants to experience this illness, though to certain extent money loss may not count. So, this is the reason why, eating good food is very important and at any point, one must not skip meals and must develop good eating habits, which is very important for the body. One may think, I do not need to eat now, but it's not you that need food, but the body needs food, that is more important thing that we must know.

Balanced diet: Having regular meals is very important as we spoke earlier, but at the same time, having all types of vitamins intake is also very important as it nourishes the body. Our diet should contain all types of foods, fruits, vegetables, meat, nuts, pulses, juices, etc..., everything should be balanced and not skip any of these. I know a person who used to eat a healthy food on a regular basis. Healthy food does not mean fast food and processed foods. Fast food and junk food is very taste to the mouth, but they do not give nutrition to the body and in fact, cause harm. Lack of fruits and vegetables intake will lead to different diseases and, if not taken on a long run, can lead to death.

At the right time: Food is something that needs to cooked properly and eaten in TIME. Timing of the food is very important because our body is so regulated that it needs diet in proper time. I might say, I am too busy with my work, so I will eat my lunch by 5 in the evening or breakfast at 11 or 12 o' clock, but body will not accept it. Suppose, I am working night shift and I eat dinner in right time and during the day time, I spent time in sleeping only and skip meals, then also, body will not accept the fact that it missed some diet. It is not I who needs to decide about food and its timings, but the body. It is the human body that keeps the timings very well. We need to remember that we are only using human body or in other words, we are being clothed with human body and it knows what it wants and it is a like a pet that needs to catered and cared for. It knows it time, birth, death, etc... all the details. We must remember to feed it in proper time and not say, I do not have time. If we say, I do not have time, then, it will say, even, I will not give you time in the future and will say goodbye to us. Hence, the meals that we feed regularly to the human body must be given on a priority basis, no matter the circumstances are.

Maintain good sleep and exercise: Now, along with eating good food and balanced diet and eating in TIME, it is also important to maintain good sleep and exercise. One thing, I can say, human body is a like child, it needs everything to be taken care in time, do not make the body suffer in any way, because if we do not take of our body, it will in return give us great gifts of illness and diseases, which are the experiences that we must go through even if we do no like. The experiences of being ill or becoming sick is more painful than being healthy and good condition. So, its better to say no to disease. We need to maintain good exercise level or at least walk a few steps and give some sort of movement for the body. I mean, come out of the comfort zone and move the body, though its quite taxing in the beginning, but later, will get used to it and will give good results. Good sleep also is necessary. Deprivation of sleep causes unnecessary diseases and illnesses. One must give sufficient rest for the body, so that it gets recharged for better activities the next day.

Good hygiene practices: Human body is a gift from GOD, let's take an example, your father or your best friend gives you good gift, let's say, very expensive mobile, so, what do you do with that. Usually speaking, we handle the mobile with extreme care and in other words, by taking care of that gift, we are giving great respect to the giver of the gift. So, in the same way, human body is a gift from GOD, and by not taking care of this body or ill treating it or by committing suicide, in a way, you are disrespecting the giver of the gift. Human body is a very expensive gift and its priceless.

So, it is essential that we take good care of the body, by practicing good hygiene habits, some of them are,

- Washing the body regularly.
- Cleaning your teeth.
- Going to the washroom regularly.
- Washing hair and keeping yourself clean and neat.
- Taking good rest
- Eating food in time.

Thus, these are some of the important key points that we need to follow in order for us to stay healthy and be happy.

<u>Importance of heath supplements</u>

Human race is a highly developed race and is a developing race, but in terms of food, the quality of food that we eat is slowly deteriorating. In other words, we are not really getting good nutrients in our food today as compared to the past few years ago. Today, our food is a mixture of chemicals and pesticides, and of course, very tasty food, but does not give us sufficient amount of energy to our human body, that is the main issue today and for future generations to come. These days, junk food has become a fashionable food and its mainly because its very tasty, but seriously speaking, it's a waste food that should never be considered for eating. It is not good for health and it does not provide good nutrients or any vitamins and it harms one's health very badly.

Health supplements: Health supplements are alternatives or sort of replacement or additional benefits to the daily food intake. It supplies and gives needed energy and vitamins to the body. These health supplements are prepared and made out of natural elements and materials. One might still ask the question, why natural health supplements, why not consider eating right kind of food.

Here, the question is, food today is being contaminated with so many chemicals and we are not able to get right kind of vitamins and proteins that human body needs today. These days, people are even making and producing food out of plastic, and foods such as rice, vegetables eggs, etc.. and one cannot really make out whether the food is plastic or real food, and perhaps, in the coming future, no wonder, if one has to sustain oneself purely from plastic food and depend on health supplements for proteins and vitamins. We might have to see real rice and vegetables in exhibitions and museums, which is even pathetic to even think of.

Trillion-dollar business: Obviously, due to lack of proteins and vitamins in our regular food, human race will have to depend on health supplements and the demand for these supplements will grow tremendously in the coming future. It is estimated that this industry will boom and will make profits in trillion dollars in the coming decade. People have become aware of their health issues and wish to maintain good health. Lot of awareness has creeped among individuals about their health and people today are being health conscious. More than that, health supplements are easily available today in the market and there are no side effects in these health supplements and anyone can take these pills without going to the doctor. It is like, many individuals are avoiding themselves going to the doctor and trying to diagnose themselves through their own individual channels, and today, Internet is the biggest help for anyone. They can easily search anything on Internet or social media and help is easily available for their solutions.

People used to experience and suffer lifestyle disease like diabetes, obesity, high blood pressure, etc…, but today, the trend has changed. People are better informed about all the issues, may not be educated, but well informed in advance through current technology. This is the reason why, preventive measures are being taken by everyone and health consciousness is building up in the minds of many people today and as a result, self-medication has become very common these days.

With regards to health supplements, many companies and even government is spending so much huge amount of money for further research, whereby, companies can make good health supplements to increase the health of people. Consumer attitude is very positive regarding dietary supplements with added health and wellness benefits.

Rising demand of organic products in U.S., Argentina, and Australia has forced regulatory bodies to frame supportive policies to increase production output for organic foods which will result in reduced application of dietary supplements in the upcoming years.

Asia Pacific was the second largest market, accounting for 31% of total share in 2018. Rising sales of royal jelly, green juice, blueberries, black vinegar, and chlorella in Japan owing to increasing demand of natural products is expected to propel the demand for nutritional supplements over the forecast period.

Global dietary supplements market was valued at USD 101.38 billion in 2018, registering a CAGR of 6.9%, during the forecast period (2019-2024).The dietary supplements market is preliminarily driven by the paradigm shift toward preventive health management practices, amid rising healthcare costs and increasing burden of lifestyle diseases. Based on product type, the vitamin segment is steadily growing, whereas the fatty acid segment represents the fastest growing supplement segment due to the popularity of omega-3-based supplements. Asia-Pacific is the fastest growing region in the dietary supplements market, driven by major investment opportunities especially for herbal and Ayurveda extract-based products.

Focus on Preventive Health Management: The global marketplace has witnessed a paradigm shift from curative practices to preventive management in healthcare, making it a prime growth factor for the market studied. Healthcare as an industry contributes extensively to the overall economy. Emphasis on care management, focus on paying for value, and rising general inflation are major factors influencing the healthcare cost. Population in the United States, Europe, and Japan is aging, prompting consumers to seek a variety of dietary supplements for maintaining and enhancing the overall health and well being.

Sources: https://www.mordorintelligence.com/industry-reports/dietary-supplement-market

Good Food versus mood swings

Food has lot of influence on your moods, thinking, and health. Suppose, for example, I have not eaten food the whole day and by evening, I am hungry, then, naturally, my thought patterns will vary, mood swings, headache will come, etc.., so, all these symptoms will arise and will affect my behavior. The kind of food that we eat has a great influence on the effect of our thinking. Suppose, after a whole days of fasting or not having food at all for some reason or the other, one usually wishes to have good plate of meals at the end of the day and it that does not happen, it causes a bit of irritation in the mind, though physically not displayed or exhibited. At the same time, in a normal scenario, you have gone to star hotel or attended a function where good food is served, you will eat with great enthusiasm and happiness, and by the end of the meal, you will have a great feeling of satisfaction and happiness in your mind and in your heart, and this is what I mean by influencing of thoughts and mood with the kind of die that we eat. At the time of illness, human body does not feel comfortable fond is not at ease at all and mood swings will be different during those times of sickness.

Mood swings: Human body does indeed require certain elements for its sustenance. Many, for whatever reasons, ignore the importance of having good diet at the right time. On a daily basis, the tissues must be supplied with the right kind of body building materials unlike in the plastering a house, if you mix less than enough lime in the sand or just make a plaster of sand and water and smooth it on your walls, in a very short run, the plaster will begin to fall off, although you may not have noticed anything wrong with its appearance. In the same way, human body decays when not plastered with the right kind of blood containing the correct kind and quantity and quality of building materials. The body begins to lose vigor, tissues become weak, skin begins to wrinkle, and cells begin to lose its building power. So, its extremely important that you supply your body with proper building material such as breakfast, lunch and dinner in such a way that you are making sure that you are giving your body proper sustenance. Hence, it is more essential to develop and maintain the powers of digestion, oxygenation, chemicalization, elimination, crystallization, metabolism, and assimilation. Food materials may be classified as proteins, fats, carbohydrates, water, mineral salts, and vitamins. Your food during the day should consist of adequate proportions of these materials and elements.

Building materials:

Proteins consist of highly complex combinations of amino acids containing chiefly carbon, hydrogen, nitrogen, oxygen and Sulphur. Proteins are needed for the construction of all living cells. Sources of animal protein are meat, fish, milk, cheese and eggs. Vegetable proteins are found in protein flour, legumes and nuts.

Fats are energy producing and consist of oily matter found in vegetables and animal foods. These lubricate the cells and are extremely necessary for oiling the joints and limbs in order to prevent tear, wear and uncomfortable friction.

Carbohydrates are used as fuel and consist of compounds of carbon, hydrogen, and oxygen, including sugar, starch and cellulose. They are found in grain products, potatoes, peas and beans, corn, tapioca, honey, sweet fruits.

Water is the carrier which transports food elements to the cells and carries away waste products.

Mineral salts have great tissue building powers. They are found in all fruits and vegetables, especially leafy vegetables and greens.

Vitamins regulate various metabolic processes and are essential to the nutrition of vertebrates. Vitamins are abundantly present in all raw fruits and vegetables. Nature is the best cook and she prepares all vegetables and fruits with ultraviolet rays and distilled water.

Blood building foods: Tomato juice, lemon or lemon juice. Lemon is the best disinfectant and it kills many gems in the stomach.

Milk, cottage cheese, channa, coconut, marrow, squash, pineapple and nuts are good for bone health.

Olive oil, almond butter, nut margarine, nut butters, cream and butter are good lubricating foods.

All forms of nuts, milk, and fish are good for the brain development. Feeding the skin pores with fresh pure cream or using coconut milk on face, hands, and arms before retiring is very effective for skin. Here, the caution, overindulgence in the use of sex energy will destroy the beauty of the skin and loveliness of the face. Bananas, nuts, butter milk, cream, fresh and dried fruits are very good and are energy building foods.

In short, food is very essential for human body, the better kind of food that we eat, the better kind of health we can preserve. Our thought process, vitality, energy, enthusiasm, sharpness, brilliance, etc.. all depend on the kind of food that we eat. Hence, one must always consider eating good food to keep our bodies healthy.

Expectations of an outstanding employee

By birth, no one is born with extraordinary talents; all of us are born with an empty mind and with a fewer talents and capabilities. We pick up many things and learn as we grow older that are required for the livelihood; the only difference is someone picks up and learns faster and someone picks up and learns slow. No one becomes a superpower or outstanding person overnight.

Success and failure basically go hand in hand. Success gives us a sense of joy and pride, and failure discourages and depresses us, but we should not forget that in the battle of life, failures do come. In that case, we should not lose heart and give up trying again. Man is imperfect, so he often stumbles in life. Misfortunes try him, as fire tries gold.

In the field of medical transcription, many come into the field with great hopes and aspirations. In short, when we enter into the field, we do not become outstanding overnight. In the field of medical transcription, some of us fail continuously in spite of best efforts. As the saying goes, failure is the stepping stone to success, we should keep trying again and again without getting discouraged. We must study the causes of our failures, and realize our defects. It will surely help us in achieving success in our attempts. Failure therefore is not a hindrance, but a help, not a bane, but a boon. Life is a sum total of experiences and failures. It adds to our experiences and opens our eyes.

If we look into history, nothing great has ever been achieved without consistent effort in the face of seemingly insurmountable difficulties. A child for instance can seldom learn to walk, without making sustained and sincere efforts in the process tumbling and falling down a number of times. His failures never deter him to stop standing again. The doggedness in the child's resolve lies in making any number of attempts to stand up and walk whatever be the pain or fear of fall.

Thus, outstanding MTs are not born. MTs need to learn continuously with great patience and must keep trying, but never give up at any point. Why do I say that, here are few examples,

Albert Einstein did not speak until he was four and did not read until he was seven, and his teachers and parents thought he was mentally handicapped, slow and anti-social. But he caught on pretty well in the end, winning the Nobel Prize and changing the face of modern physics.

Michael Jordan Most people wouldn't believe that a man often lauded as the best basketball player of all times was actually cut from his high school basketball team. 'I have failed over and over and over again in my life, and that is why I succeeded.

Walt Disney, today Disney rakes in billions from merchandise, movies and theme parks around the world, but Walt Disney himself had a bit of a rough start. He was fired by a newspaper editor because, "he lacked imagination and had no good ideas. After that, Disney started a number of businesses that didn't last too long and ended with bankruptcy and failure. He kept plugging along, however, and eventually found a recipe for success that worked.

We need to understand that in order to gain success, and to become an outstanding MT, we need to learn some traits and develop some skills, which will help in achieve better results and to become an outstanding MT.

1. **Sincerity**. Be sincere in your efforts and actions. Don't try to deceive or impress others. Be yourself. Be enthusiastic about what you do. Show it. Be committed to work completely with strong determination.

2. **Sound judgement**. In the field of medical transcription, we must have sound judgement and ability to think differently to make right decisions at the right moment.

3. **Knowledge**. Knowledge is the key to open the door ignorance. We need to update ourselves with everything. We need to read lots and lots of literature like articles, books related to medicine and general knowledge, which will enhance power of understanding and vocabulary.

4. **Listening skills and reasoning**. Here, we need to understand one thing; we are not typists who keep tying whatever the dictator dictates. We need to reason out what the doctor says, why he says, and then we need to

transcribe. There is a difference between transcription and typing. We need to be very cautious about every sentence, every word, and we need to make sure that it makes some sense.

5. **Feedbacks**. Going through errors is one of the important things that every MT should do. We need to keep correcting errors that we make and update with the new terminology.   It is another way of correcting ourselves where we often commit errors and falter. We must try and learn new terminology that we encounterseveryday, which will help improve our vocabulary.

6. **Attitude** is one of the important trait that we need to nurture. It is always necessary to develop positive attitude towards others and towards our work. For example, H-A-R-D-W-O-R-K scores 8+1+18+4+23+15+18+11 = 98%; K-N-O-W-L-E-D-G-E scores 11+14+15+23+12+5+4+7+5 = 96%; A-T-T-I-T-U-D-E scores 1+20+20+9+20+21+4+5 = 100.

7. **Perseverance**. Successful medical transcriptionists have to have perseverance. Perseverance is the ability to

keep doing something with the knowledge that your efforts will pay off in the end. In the field of medical transcription, there are constant setbacks that can deter a professional and affect one's motivation. We should always keep one thing in mind, "Never give up even if we fail n-number of times, we should keep trying."

We should have love towards work rather than hard work because anyone is ready to do hard work either manual or mental. If we really love our work, we can certainly achieve better results. I believe, with all these aspects, one should become outstanding in the industry.

Idea of being an entrepreneur

Becoming an entrepreneur is a challenging task because it is a new stream and new adventure. Everyone basically searches for a good job and try to build up good career by completing number of courses that would aid him or her to fetch better income prospectus. Job is always a secured and safe thing one can think of where once a month is over, one can expect returns of his or her hard work without delay. All of us basically want a better job with better salary and with good figures of income. These days, private jobs are more lucrative than government jobs, and in fact, government jobs are very hard to get these days and one need to wait for a whole lifetime to get a government job. In the private sector also, if one exhibits good skills and proficient at work, one can get good income. Basically speaking, only a few people think of doing a business on their own. It definitely involves lot of risk, and yet, some dare and takes chances and risks and some succeed.

Why entrepreneur: Becoming an entrepreneur is always interesting, but one must have passion and desire towards becoming an entrepreneur. When it comes to job, which many people think it as a secured one, always has limitations. One cannot really settle down in life properly unless one is into very high paying jobs. These days, as the cost of living is very high due to inflation and to meet the demands of life, one must workout in developing some sort of income plans, otherwise, it will become extremely difficult to maintain better living conditions.

Becoming an entrepreneur is doing business independently. There are many advantages if one chooses to become an entrepreneur. You can decide how much income you want and you are the owner of your own business. You do not have to follow any rules, you can create your own rules. Initially speaking, perhaps, one might encounter with challenges at the start of your business, but as the time goes on, definitely, one will gain prosperity and income.

Business mind: In life, there are two ways of thinking, doing the work by yourself and asking someone to do the work for yourself. First, working full-time as an employee. As far as I know, there are many people who work two jobs in order to get better income to meet the cost of living. In other words, working almost 16 to 18 hours a day, which would put tremendous amount of pressure on physical body and would cause mental stress due to lack of sleep and pressure from work. As a result of this, one would lose one's personal life. Basically speaking, everyone in this world has only 24 hours, but how one makes use of this 24 hours is what matters most. Business people always do not think of working, but rather thinks of relaxing and spent most of their time in entertainment, but here, puzzling question might come to everyone, how they will get millions and billions of dollars. The answer is very simple, they will not work, but will employee people to do the work for them and instead of working 8 to 12 hours of work, business people will employ 10 people, let's say, and get the work done and pay them accordingly. Here, what makes them so strong and determined about their business ideas, what inspires them and what motivates them. Basically, they do not like to work hard and they believe in, what is called innovative ideas of doing business, which will fetch them millions of dollars.

Becoming an entrepreneur is, however, is a challenge and it is not a secured job, but will gain and experience lot of freedom. Many people dream about being an entrepreneur, starting their own business, working for themselves and living the good live. Very few, however, will actually take the plunge and put everything they have got into being their own boss. Everyone is an entrepreneur. The only skill you need to be an entrepreneur, an ability to fail, an ability to have ideas, to sell those ideas, to execute on those ideas, and to be persistent. Even if you fail, must learn to move on for the next adventures. You should strongly desire to reach that position that you always wanted. In other words, you must redesign your thought pattern and program your mind and your mind will in fact pushes you to where you want to be.

Many of us go to temples as we are studying or after completing studies, and pray for a good job and to go to other countries for better income. Here, my question is, do you need a job or an income, what you need in life. It is like, you must be able to give salaries to people. The most confusing question is, need a job or an income. All of us tend to think of a job that gives us a secured income. Think of an income rather than a job because job is a limited word and has a scope that does not spread its roots beyond like a business. So, must start thinking in terms of getting income through some business or the other. Start paying salaries and get things done for you and you will automatically become an entrepreneur and a businessman and life will change.

Business ideas: I remember years back working in one of the reputed companies very hard, working so hard and doing night shifts. In the morning hours, as colleagues and friends, used to go for a sip of tea and/or coffee. We used to have a chat with the tea maker and he was so free with us because we regularly visit him for a cup of tea. We just casually asked him how much he was making. We were puzzled to hear his income. He was so young and he opened the branch of tea shop in another place. We could not believe that he was getting income of ten of us at that age. Years back, I did not understand the thought of that entrepreneur. So, there are many ideas today to start your own business, but only thing, one must know how to implement and execute them in appropriate way. Working as an entrepreneur is something and having an idea of becoming an entrepreneur is another thing. It is a passion and not an idea in the mind.

Thought pattern: Having a strong mind like a businessman is very important and one must have passion to do business. A thought of a business is very important and not the size of a business. In order to achieve and go ahead with that thought, one must have strong motivation and courage to go ahead and stand on your decision because there will be so many distractions and discouragements that come on the way. One must know how to face these challenges courageously rather than get disappointed. So, it is very essential to have a positive attitude and mind to achieve what you need and want. One must avoid negative attitude. Believe and be strong in what you do. I do not believe in having dreams, dreams are not that you should have. You should consider yourself to be just there, the position that you want and need that is important. Have a clear-cut picture of what you need and want. Have a business plan, learn the tactics, strategies and discuss with experts and think wisely before you take any step.

Importance of continuing education

We must learn to update ourselves. We must not stop learning. Learning is a continuous process. These days, we have so much material and literature available, either in physical form or in digital form in the form of internet, e-books and so on. Many would say, learning and education is money and without which we do not need education or study or learning. Generally speaking, money plays a huge role in anything that we do, but of course, I believe, during the journey of learning, down the road, some brilliant idea might come and show you the way for income generation. With regards to creating revenues, it might take some time for some people and for some, it is a quick process, and for some people, it could be a long process, but whatever the process, never give up, keep learning, and after all, learning equals money.

In the words of Aristotle, anything that we have to learn to do we learn by the actual doing of it. According to Plate, he said that each person should do the job that they are best suited for, and as a result of your continuous efforts, you will reap fruits out of it.

To keep yourself updated: There are two ways of living human life, one is, get the desired job of your choice or business, whichever provides better income for you and be happy with that and not bothered by the happenings are the world. Another way is, doing the same thing, but here, updating oneself with the latest events, trends, and knowing many interesting things. Latest trends, I do not mean, only related to politics or society, but learning and enhancing your knowledge, just for the sake of gaining knowledge because by this way, one gets updated with the latest knowledge and does not lag behind.

Knowledge gives you confidence: Knowledge give you confidence and self-respect. In other words, you are not a frog in the well, not knowing as to what is happening around the world. In the olden days, let's say, around 100 or two hundred years back, there were no proper schools or colleges during that time. Wealthy families usually used to hire tutors to teach and educate their kids with different subjects and activities. If we seriously examine the lifestyle of their kids, they had to learn all the subjects, Maths, philosophy, science, music, arts, painting and so on and their schedule was fixed from morning to evening and only on Sundays, they were given a bit of freedom, perhaps to play. In other words, they focused on all round learning and development, which is most essential.

New ideas: As we keep reading new literature and books, we gain lot of insights and knowledge, and as a result of which we get new ideas and new thoughts and new insights. This newness will definitely prompt and will help us to create something new, to write something new and for better living conditions.

Learning is money: It is the proven fact that learning means money. Suppose, a job requirement is posted in the newspaper or on internet and basically, qualifications will be mentioned in the job post or ads and that particular job requires people who hold post-graduation program. Suppose, if one does not have that degree, then, obvious thought would arise in his or her mind to complete the post-graduation program in order to enhance further growth options in his or her career. Learning is something that does not stop at any age. We have to keep learning in order to fit ourselves properly in the society. In short, learning equals lot of money.

Never stop learning: Learning is something we should not stop. It is like breathing, we stop breathing only with death. In the same way, learning is a must. I remember an old woman completing her PhD at the age of 80. So, what she will do with that PhD at that age and people might laugh her, but it is the attitude towards learning and wanting to learn new things is very important. It is about consideration of knowing new things. Aristotle, the great philosopher, was imprisoned for 27 long years and was kept in one of the cells of the castle at that time because his writings were stirring and kings felt his writings to be a threat. So, during one of his days in prison just before his death, he heard someone singing and Aristotle felt the tube to be heavenly, and so, he wanted to learn the tune. So, he asked his mate to teach him the tune, but his jail mate told him, anyways, you are going to be executed tomorrow, why do you want to learn now and what are you going to do with this new song. Aristotle said, it does not matter, I have passion for learning, I will die singing this new song and this adds to my knowledge bank and at least, I do not wish to die as an ignorant person, but rather a wise man that is knowledgeable.

After all, learning is a passion: Learning and gaining knowledge must entail passion. Suppose, someone tells you that it is good to read books, and you might start reading books or trying to learn something just because someone has told you, but that enthusiasm will not last long because that enthusiasm and energy should be deeply rooted in your mind and heart. It is like, you must be madly love with learning and knowledge, passion to learn something new.

Go beyond the text books: Being narrow minded does not help at all and in fact, leaves one in darkness and just believing blindly to everything and anything. We are trapped in the thoughts of narrow mindedness and god, religion and society are the powers that walls and block us to go beyond these walls. Hence, it is very important that one must learn and understand different concepts and must think out of the box, which can help one to realize who she or he is.

Learning from one another

Learning from one another is a good thought and very important and essential because we cannot consider ourselves as perfect beings. We do not possess complete knowledge and no one can know everything and that is why, it is important that we learn from one another. If we consider ourselves as full, then it is wrong, because none of us living on this planet can possess full knowledge, we need to learn from each other.

Learning does not occur by chance, it must be sought for with ardor and attended to with diligence." —Abigail Adams

Pooling knowledge: Cricket players or any other players, if we examine them closely, each player after their match, they review their match and couch directs them and gives them feedback. Couch advises the players where he or she went wrong and what is the best method and strategy of the game for him and her. This is how, each player is trained and learns from others. Every player also watches the game of others in order to identify their strengths and weaknesses. This is how learning process takes place.

Brainstorming: Brainstorming is a method that many companies and organization use in order to obtain better solutions for problem solving and in order to get better ideas for the growth of organization. Usually, a team of members are assembled in the conference hall and each one is invited to throw their ideas and solution to the issues that they are currently facing. I may know something or some information that you may not know or be aware of and you possess knowledge that I do not know, which I need to learn from you. With this method, everyone gives their share of information and that is chronicled and scripted and would be reviewed in order to get better results for the companies and organizations.

Group discussions: Group discussion is another method of interacting with one another. This technique is used in number of organizations and educational institutions. Group of about 5 to 10 members are gathered like in a round table conference. A situation is created or specific topic is given to discuss upon and each member of the group will need to contribute by sharing and discussing upon the given topic. It is basically a healthy interaction that should take place and not a heated argument where each one will start fighting with each other. The purpose of group discussion is to interact with one another whereby, each one gets to learn from one another.

Seminars: Seminars and conferences are held across different places on different subjects and topics. Prominent speaker is present and gives a powerful presentation and gives good output and shares lot of information. So much of interaction would take place between speakers and audience whoever is attending the seminar. There is a great scope to interact with one another and get to know about each other and knowledge. This enhances growth in their careers and to get new clients for their business.

Library: Library is a general term that is used, both for physical library, which contains numerous amount of books that are placed in a physical building and digital library where millions of books are available online. Library means bank of knowledge. These millions of books are written by wise people who have done a lot of research on various subjects.

Never give up on a dream just because of the time it will take to accomplish it, the time will pass anyway. –Earl Nightingale

Careers in electronic medical records

Medical transcription is the hottest career option due to its inflow of number of jobs and potentiality of income. Many people are the world pursued this career and had earned lot of income through this career. Medical transcription is a healthcare stream, which would last for a long time. At one time, the field witnessed glorious outcome, but right now due to increasing cost of living and with the stagnant revenues from medical transcription, life is becoming tougher for many individuals who are already in this field. However, world is not an end and moreover, medical transcription has gotten into the next level, and that being is EMR/EHR, electronic medical records/electronic healthcare records, which gives a scope for better earning potential for employees and gives a scope for doctors to cut down the pricing of outsourcing.

As of today, we can see and observe, the traditional way transcription is slowly disappearing and EMR is being showcased as a stage of career option. People who have got acclimatized to the traditional way of transcription, might find it a bit hard to get used to new way of transcription, it is the new cup that takes away the comfort level of being listened to all the time. Traditional transcription is like depending on everything and it is like we are told what we need to do, but when it comes to new level of transcription, its collection of choices and options, and based on those options, we need to make the final decision and stick with it. It is in fact, nice cup of coffee because it improves our creativity and potential for earnings.

Medical scribe: It is essentially a personal assistant to the physician, performing documentation process, gathering information for the patient's visit, and partnering with the physician to deliver the pinnacle of efficient patient care. It is like working very closely with the physician and helping the physicians to manage and do the documentation process.

Types of transcription: Since years, we have had many types of transcription that is available in the market. Transcription is very essential in order to make the data available for clients. Some of the known types of transcription are,

- ➢ General transcription
- ➢ Business transcription

- Legal transcription
- Audio transcription
- Video transcription
- Cinema transcription
- Interviews transcription
- Sermon transcription
- Academic transcription and the list can go on.....

EMR/EHR: Electronic medical records, it is a new method of career, it's a new cup to drink, but its very interesting. This type of transcription is completely nonvoice based. In this type of job, the doctor does not dictate anything. Thanks for the evolution of artificial intelligence and because of which, we have voice recognition software available in the market. With the use of voice recognition, we are able to record the conversation that runs between the doctor and the patient and the details are recorded and typed automatically with the help of the software. Now, this is called raw data. The doctor basically needs the fresh data that is necessary to submit to the insurance companies. Here, the role of experienced transcriptionists is that they need to clean the data and get keywords and key phrases that are necessary and required for physician, so that it would aid for billing and legal process.

These days, many companies are working in catering this type of EMR work and many are showing interest in working in EMR process. The sole reason is, it gives great opportunity for doctors to cut down the pricing of medical transcription, which is an old and traditional method. On the other hand, it gives scope for employees to focus on better earnings and gives potential to earn more within the limited time, the basic working hours in which each employee used to work earlier in traditional medical transcription and in fact, it helps people to double their earnings.

Do not limit yourself or build walls around you, always, dream big and expand yourselves and wish for good things to come to you and it will indeed come to you.

How to repair toxic relationships

Today's climate of constraint and competition has a way of increasing tensions and reducing the energy available to work on the goals and objectives of the organization. Delivery of programs and services suffer, as organizations become concerned with survival. Tensions and conflicts tend to build up in a climate of constraint, with unrealistic expectations and inadequate resources, that is the do more with less syndrome. Conflict is constructive when it results in clarification, serves as a release to pent-up emotions and stress. When people understand each other's needs and use the conflict to build cooperation and trust. Conflict is neither good nor bad. It is part of human nature and to be expected when humans interact. Conflict can provide opportunities to learn new skills, develop problem-solving abilities and infuse energy. If unresolved, conflict grows, so it is important to recognise symptoms and address a conflict early before it become destructive.

Some of the key features of conflict are,

Conflict is inevitable

Conflict does not have to result in winners and losers

In conflict, both parties tend to believe that their opinion is correct

Too often, both parties see themselves innocent victims who represent the side of truth and fairness

Too often, both parties perceive all destructive acts carried out by others completely blind to identical acts carried out by self or those on my side.

Difference of perceptions of conflicts:

Conflict is unnatural

Something is wrong with people who are causing violence and conflict

Conflict is part of daily life

Conflict may be interesting

Conflict may be positive and constructive

Conflict is a virtual necessity for growth and change, for individuals and groups.

Conflicts can only be understood within the context in which it occurs

Conflict should be expressed as soon as possible in order for it to disappear

Emotions often cloud the mind and therefore, should not be expressed

Emotions disable logical thinking and weaken the position of the parties

People have to express their emotions before they can go on with resolving the conflict

Causes of conflict: Conflicts have various reasons, such as material goods, principles, territory, communication, policies, personalities and so on. We can categorise them as instrumental conflicts, conflicts of interest and personal/relational conflicts. Instrumental conflicts concern goals, means, procedures and structures. Conflicts of interest concern the distribution of means such as money, time, staff and space. Personal conflicts are about questions of identity and self-image and important aspect of relationships.

Resolution: Addressing conflict early allows the individuals involved in the conflict to control the outcome and their own destiny. Negotiation offers most control over the conflict and the outcome because the parties work together to resolve the conflict. If the parties cannot work together to resolve the conflict, they may use mediation, that is a neutral third party who helps the conflicting parties solve their issues. The mediator does not solve the conflicts, but helps and guides them to reach to logical and meaningful conclusions.

Each person has the right to be treated with respect, the right to have and to express feelings, opinions and wants, the right to be listened to and taken seriously by others. Too often in conflict situations, these rights get ignored. Assertive communication is critical in resolving conflicts, so that all parties win. There are two important skills in effective communication, assertive behaviour, that is clearly expressing what you feel and saying what you want and active listening that is listening with understanding and supportive way. There is variety of behavioural styles of communication, passive, aggressive, passive-aggressive, and assertive. Although any of these behaviours may be appropriate in certain circumstances, the assertive style offers the most effective behaviour for dealing with and reducing conflicts.

During the mediation process, it is very important to know your personal and cultural values because they have an impact. If the values and cultural traditions differ from yours, it is important to get to know them before you can even start and prepare yourself by consulting an expert and how to deal with these types of disputes. One thing, you must keep in mind is that, there are lot of emotions that get involved in relationships. One must have a clear picture of the problems and/or conflicts, and then only, one must think of understanding each one and their issues.

The collaborating mode of conflict resolution is high in assertiveness and high in cooperation. Collaboration has been described as putting an idea on top of an idea in order to achieve the best solution to a conflict. The best solution is defined as a creative solution to the conflict that would not have been generated by a single individual. With such a positive outcome for collaboration, some people will profess that the collaboration is always the best conflict mode to use.

Sometimes, it is better to let go of your position for a moment. Think about what the other person needs and wants. Work with others to identify underlying concerns and issues. Consider all the options and how all the parties stand to benefit from each one. Focus on your own concerns. Give yourself time to gather data that support your problems, your reasons and how and why they matter. Take a deep breath, calmly state your concerns and why they are so important.

Information is the key to success in negotiation

Everyone is a negotiator. It is an everyday occurrence. Life is an endless series of interactions that require negotiation. You are confronted daily with countless situations in which you are called upon to negotiate, to reach an agreement, or to resolve an conflict or difference of option. For example, negotiating at bedtime with children regarding holidays or vacation destination with family and/or friends, the issue is not whether you negotiate, but rather how effective you are. Negotiation is a skill that can be improved with practice. Traditionally speaking, it has been a confrontational, for example, talk rough and see how much you can get. This negative attitude to negotiation is deeply embedded in many cultures. Most books and courses on negotiation focus on the adversarial relationships.

Power is a widely misunderstood term which often carries negative connotations. In negotiation, power is positive use of resources to achieve worthwhile goals and influence people and events. It is a subjective mental force, the extent of which is determined largely by perception, both yours and the other party's. In other words, if you think, you have it, you have it. If you think, you do not have it, you do not have it.

Successful negotiation requires that you draw on every imaginable information source,

Opinions from experts

The known facts and background of the situation

Personalities and sensitivities of the other people

The timeframe

Behavioural and verbal cues

The negotiating environment

The authority of the other party has to finalize matters of all the information sources, cues are the most important and often most difficult to recognize.

Part of the success in gathering information is to recognize that negotiating is not an event, but a process.

Web of tension: This involves two elements, time and organizational issues and pressures. Time usually means deadlines, both yours and others. The others may conceal its deadline, but it has one all the same. Organizational pressure refers to the strength and support of the negotiator's organization and how it affects the negotiator's ability to take risks and vary approaches. The more support a negotiator gathers, the more his team can accomplish as a group. A skilled negotiator not only knows how to use techniques, but also how to recognize them in others.

Basic skills required to become a negotiator,

Understanding yourself

Defining outcomes

Understanding and defining positions

Framing and reframing

People make commitments to individuals, not institutions, so personalized transactions have a greater chance to succeed.

In personalizing the negotiation, it helps to develop a good relationship with the other party before you negotiate, although this is not always possible.

Move towards your objective gradually, making concessions one at a time.

Information gathering also plays a vital role in negotiation because it is always said that knowledge is power.

However, in spite of all these factors, knowledge plays a key role in negotiation. Knowledge is power and the more knowledge one possesses and is able to accumulate about others, the better chances are for victory.

Building a house on sand

We cannot take a decision based on emotions because emotions do not sustain for long. Any decision pertaining to anything must be taken with clear mind and strong will. It is like the story from the bible, building a house on sand and not on rock. Everyone then who hears these words of mine and does them will be like a wise man who built his house on the rock. And the rain fell, and the floods came, and the winds blew and beat on that house, but it did not fall, because it had been founded on the rock. And everyone who hears these words of mine and does not do them will be like a foolish man who built his house on the sand. And the rain fell, and the floods came, and the winds blew and beat against that house, and it fell, and great was the fall of it.

We cannot take words in the literal sense because building a house on sand is possible now with the latest technology. I mean to say, emotions do not last long and they are short lived and they do not have strong foundation for good base. Hence, based on certain emotions, we cannot make any decisions. It is said that when we are emotionally not balanced or undergoing some emotional turmoil, it is better to stay away from making any wise decisions or better to go for counselling for help and to come out of this emotional status.

Weak foundation: Emotions and feelings come and go and they are like passing clouds. They do not really last long. We see many times that people challenging others, that if I cannot do this or achieve that, I will change my name. So, it's really funny, what is the necessity of changing the name and believe me, it's very difficult to change names legally these days, bit expensive and long process. These kinds of statements are made out of pure emotion and when that emotion subsides, the challenging statements also weakness and will not have strength. Then, later on, that person might begin to think, oh god, why did I challenge that person. It is like making and take a decision about unrealistic goals and dreams. Hence, one must try and avoid these kinds of situations and when in stress or emotionally effected, it is better to take some time off to relax first rather than just bursting out with emotions.

Strong foundation: Here, we are not connected with any emotions. Decision is made on anything by doing some research, consulting a wise person and without any bias opinions on any other people. Generally speaking, emotions are always displayed and interpreted as wild animals in dreams. Whenever we get wild animals attacking us in our dreams, it means that we are not in control of our emotions and feelings. I do not mean to say that emotions are bad and either way, emotions are good or bad, but when it comes to wise decision making, we should keep emotions and feelings and challenging statements and words aside.

Brainstorming: It is a process and method used in many organizations these days and is highly productive. No one is equipped with full knowledge and we need to learn from one another. I know something which the person does not know about it. I may not know some information, which the other person is aware of. It is basically sharing of knowledge, communicating valuable information with one and other. Digital marketing is the best example of this and through digital marketing, for example, blogging or YouTube channel, lot of information is thrown through these methods. In the physicality, let us say, there are ten people sitting in conference hall, and one problem or issue is raised and everyone is asked to throw out their ideas, suggestions, and opinions. All this information is noted down, analysed, and can be used and put in productive purpose. Through digitalization, we can get much better information today. If you do not know anything, just ask Google assistant or Google, it will give answer, the most probable suggestions, so that based on these suggestions, you can make a proper decision.

Seek help from experts: We need to accept the fact that we are all emotional beings, however, when it comes to making a good decision, we should not depend on emotions and instead, keep emotions aside and then, make a decision. While making a good decision, there are certain factors that we need to keep in mind. We should have sound mind, both physically and mentally because even if we are sick with some illness, there will always be some tendency that our cognitive function will be very weak or even if we have lack of sleep and sleep deprivation can cause irritation and we cannot make a good decision. In any case, when it comes to decision making, it is always advisable to approach wise people, perhaps, experts for appropriate suggestions.

Clarity of thought: Financial freedom is the burning issue today and many of us want to have better income and be happy without financial difficulties. Education basically gives everyone some foundation and grounding for clarity of thought. Society and the growing up also has a great influence on developing a clarity of thought of what we need. It definitely comes with experience and having good network of friends and connections. Once we decide what we need in life, we must pen down on paper the constructive plan for the future and must try to implement it.

Do some research: We must possess passion for knowledge because learning equals lot of money. Today, in the society, we need lot of money to live as the cost of living is increasing day by day. Today, every piece of information is available on internet, we just need to ask Google of what we need and what kind of information we need. We can get lot of free courses and materials online at no cost and freely. Hence, it is up to us to decide what we need and how to go about, and thus, lot of changes we can bring out and everything is in our hands.

<u>Are you living life by choice or by chance?</u>

We all make a number of choices in life. Here, I am talking about choices and not decision. Choice is something that we take before making a final decision either by us directly or indirectly or by someone else imposes those choices on us. Suppose, as kids, we may not know what clothes to wear, the selection of food, school, holiday trips, toys, and so on, parents and others decide for us. We never had the opportunity to decide for ourselves because our mind was not well equipped to make any choices or decisions. At birth, human mind is like a blank paper, it is a new world that we have entered into, new realm of life, new adventure, which we need to explore.On a daily basis, we all make a number of choices. We are not here on earth by chance, it is by choice. We make number of choices to be happy, in facing problems, in tacking different situations, and so on. We make a number of choices from morning to evening.

Life is always not by chance, whether it is a holiday or working day, we choose the time to get up early or late, it all depends the kind of values we have for our lives. Every morning, we wake to see the world, to see the light, choice is in our hands, either to conquer the day or you let the day conquer you.

Our education: When it comes to education, as children, of course, up to tenth standard, it is a common education. Here, the question, is your mind getting equipped with knowledge to make well informed choices and decisions in your life. As a school going kid, are you getting involved with all the activities that the school is organizing or just keeping silent aside. School education is just a foundation to make a proper choice to go ahead with college studies and therefore, with a better career that suits you. Here, again, another question arises, is it really choice that you made personally after doing some research and consulting with your friends and teachers or by chance, just because everyone is going blindly, you also tend to go that way. Gathering information about future is always good, but ultimately, you need to make a good decision based on the information provided to you, from your friends, internet, teachers, parents or anyone in the society. Suppose, just because someone has suggested you to go ahead with engineering course, are you going ahead with the course or MBBS and are you really clear about the choice that you are making for yourself. The course that you have selected, do you really like the course and passionate about the path that you have chosen. Simple question one might even ask, the shirt that you are wearing, it is your choice or some one's choice. It is very important to be very clear about our choices in life. Some are very clear about their goals in life and go ahead in life without hesitation even if others tend to react and disrespect your decision and they will stand by their decision and that is very important. Schools, college education is only a theoretical knowledge, and it only gives you certain limitations and one must be really very good in doing some research when it comes to any subject. In other words, one must have practice knowledge and in order to gain this knowledge, you must go beyond books. It is like, you must already have practice knowledge of what course you are going to pursue because by this way, you will success very fast in life.

Career and job: Going blindly without any goal in life is not really a good choice. Many choose to pursue a good job and it all depends on what kind of studies and what kind of education and what sort of practical knowledge you have gained and made effort in order to obtain that knowledge. Some students really study very hard and score well, but many at times, they tend to fare well in jobs. Some students, who are not really dull, but have practical knowledge and they do well when it comes to jobs and in their projects. Some discontinue their studies, not because they are not interested in studies, but they are more passionate about knowledge and not education. Here, I mean, education is different and knowledge is different. One can have passion for knowledge, willingness to learn new things, desire to try out new technology and that is why, they feel college education to be a boring one. That is why, they discontinue the studies, but they are very good at their subject. So, we can call this, their dropout of college and discontinuation of studies in not by chance, but by their own personal choice. Perhaps, in the future, they will establish and run their own companies. Degrees and certificates are not the criteria to get money, but knowledge and how to get that income is very important.

Life partner: Life partner plays a very important role in life. Love or arranged marriage, make no difference in my opinion because, even in arranged marriage, there is great presence of love. The definition of marriage has changed today. In the past, couple need to live until death and it was considered to be good for society and was considered love, but today, the meaning has changed, marriage does not mean, just living together with the certification of marriage in churches, temples, or some other holy place. It means, when two people, boy and girl love each other, they decide to live together, which we call today living together or cohabitation. There is love in this kind of relationship also. Love is not just sexual relationship; it is much more beyond this. Love is understanding, patience and so on and it is not only physical, but emotional and spiritual. Some choose to get divorced soon after the marriage or after a few years of marriage, for many various reasons, one strongest reason could be for financial settlement. Some get divorced because they love each other. It is really funny when I say that, yes, they get separated because they love each other, because each one's world is completely different and it disturbs them if they live together. Hence, they decide to get separated and still continue their relationships.

Purpose of life: Many have very strong goals and aims in life. Some have small goals and small desires. Some, GOD knows, they do not even know why they are living, they live, looks like, someone tells them to live, just for the sake of living. Have a purpose in life. As a man, he will have so many desires and goals and as a woman, she will have different set of desires goals and once, they feel, all are fulfilled, they feel life as complete. One example, one teacher living in certain city, but has lost all his family, and he is very rich and has lot of property. He lost his family because of one famous and powerful person. The goal of teacher is only to take revenge whatever it could take. So, he decided to sell all his property and collected all his shares and money and made an offer, whoever kills this person who was the culprit and the cause of loss of teacher's family. And, once that is achieved, he is happy, though this is negative goal, but he felt complete by achieving this goal. Some have goals of becoming a CEO of the company and some wish to have their own house and car and bank balance, and once they reach their goals, they will feel life as complete. For some, it can be, getting a good girlfriend who is beautiful, fair in colour and so on.

Thus, each one's life is completely different from others. We have to decide which kind of life we want and make the right choice for ourselves. After all, by the end of the day, when we go to bed, we must feel and experience happiness and sense of satisfaction in life. Moreover, values also play an important role in life. And, when you turn 60 or 70 or when you know that you are nearing death, I mean, while leaving physical body, when you recollect your life, you should be able to say, that, yes, I have lived my life with great meaning and purpose and my life is complete and I am very happy about my life.

Worries and concerns, consume time and energy

The definition of success changes from person to person and it changes from country to country and from society to society and so on. Some agree by success means, earning lot of money, for some, getting a name in the society is success, for some, ranking in the highest position is success, for some getting good scores in studies is success and so on. Here, the question is, what if one does not achieve all these or any of the things that you desired for or as students, do not get ranks, are they failures in life. Failure is only thought that is wrongly misunderstood. One must take every situation and challenges as an experience. Today, getting money is considered as great success and if one does not earn money, he or she is considered a failure. So, most of us worry about how to get more money or get worried about so many things, which we do not even know. Worrying about something only burns out our energy.

A professional golfer once was trying to score more goals, but was unable to do so. So, he started getting worried and anxious. The more anxious he became the more strokes he lost on the golf course. During particularly deep meditations, he calmed himself and left his ego behind and merged with the golf course. He then began to understand golf as a metaphor for life. Then, later on, when he went to golf course to play the golf, he just did not think about winning, but just thought of enjoying the game, and as a result of it, he began scoring more goals.

"The earth is a beautiful garden and you are here to enjoy the fruits of this garden"

Past experience: As a human person, you must have gone through a tough life earlier and negative experience that would have been causing you or troubling till now. Perhaps, someone has hurt you so badly that you are unable to forgive and forget about those incidents and situations. By not able to forget and forgive them, we are only creating and developing and cultivating more negativity and storing them within us, which is very bad. Hence, it is better to get rid off this negative energy and remain peaceful. That is why, many great people whenever they face with tough people or touch situations, they try to get rid of negative emotions quickly, so that they can go ahead with their work with pleasant emotions.

Sickness: sickness can mean, physical ailments or mental conditions. One person many not feeling well and health is deteriorated for a long time. Physically, he is not comfortable with his body because of his health issues and as a result of this sickness, it causes great worry and concern mentally also. Now, he is prone to develop mental sickness also as a result of this physical illness. It is really difficult to say, to stop worrying about it, but even if you start and continue worrying and feeling sad about, nothing is going to change.

Fruits of worries:

Heart rate increases

Muscle tensions increase

We waste lot of time and thinking

Lot of energy is wasted as a result of worry

Prone to develop mental tensions

Anxiety and depression and/or heart attack

Weight loss or weight gain

Can never be happy

The Vietnamese Buddhist monk, Thick Nhat Hanh describes enjoying a good cup of tea. You must be in the present moment, mindful and aware, to enjoy the cup of tea, to savour the sweet aroma, to taste the flavour, to feel the warmth of the cup of tea. If you are ruminating about the past events or worrying about future, you will look down at your cup and the tea will be gone. You drank it, but you do not remember because you were not aware. Life is like that cup of tea. When you are not experiencing the present, when you are absorbed in the past or worried about the future, you bring great heartache and grief to yourself.

Life is really wonderful and it's a magic. Within no time, we grow up and get old. As kids, we would have enjoyed and played a lot and as teenagers, life would have been different exposure to us. Life is a process, which we always would have experienced in some way or the other. Suppose, you are at the age of 20 or 30, now, when you grow to be around 60 or 70 and look back and see how life was for you, you should feel some satisfaction, must be able to say, yes, I have lived and was very happy about my life. Pains in life is very common, but going through pain is a painful experience and it is a part of life and just because we have been experiencing pain, does not mean that we start worrying about it. Worrying does not bring any solution, it only burns more energy from us. Perhaps, at the age of 70, when you look back, you might say, oh my god, why did I worry so much, it was so stupid thing.

Adventure: Life is always uncertain; we do not know what comes next. There is no guarantee that you will do well in school or in college. You might have planned for a wealthy life and a good business, but might have failed due to so many other reasons, perhaps, that is the right business meant for you. Marriage on the other hand cannot bring complete happiness. There will so many ups and downs. You must accept whatever comes.

Every experience and every moment of life should be savoured with happiness because we are meant to experience life. If you begin to understand and savour the life, then, you will start enjoying every moment of life and all the pleasant and bad are good for you and you know well how to handle negative moments also. Live the present moment, which is very important. If you still continue worrying about the past because worry is an element of the past and why keep digging the past, which is gone and which will be gone.

Live the present moment. As greatly said by some great people, when the darkness comes, experience it, go through it, because light will definitely come because day and night are part of this beautiful life.

<u>The steps to financial freedom</u>

Have we ever wondered animals, birds, and so on, live so happily and they do not seem to be having any worries about money and what to eat now and where to stay. Does a bird that flies in the sky, ever wonders that it needs to earn lot of money in order to save for future generation. I tend to notice some birds, for example, doves or pigeons, which often comes to my apartment and keeps flying here and there. They really do not seem to be bothered about food, shelter, or anything at all. Without any of these thoughts or worries, they get everything they need for their sustenance. Human beings, peculiar race, highly intelligent beings, but we get worried about daily life, on what to eat, where to live, and we are faced with daily challenges of life. Everyday seems to be a great challenge and are in search for money, so to have a better and comfortable life and to give a better future for future generation. Financial freedom is all about making work an option. Saving enough money to quit your job forever is a huge undertaking or getting involved into job is a time pass thing.

There are so many ways we can come over these issues and/or problems. Some of the ways, I believe, have mentioned here as below,

Enhance your knowledge: Continuous education is one of the greatest and very important elements that we must possess. It is very important and healthiest habit that each one must possess. We should not stop learning. Learning means lot of wealth and lot of money. If we stop learning, then, it is the sign that we have lost hope in life. Update your knowledge, so as to keep pace with the current and present world changes that are happening around us. Keep pace with the current events and present situation where we can possibly gain more wealth.

Relax your mind and stress free: Always, relax your mind. Never feel tensed up at any time. There are so many times we face with lot of tensions and troubles, which we feel, is very difficult to go through. By getting worried or being tensed, problems would not run away from us. I know it is very difficult thing to do, but not impossible. For instance, suppose, a person is travelling on a boat and he or she does not know swimming. Suppose, something happens and he or she falls into the water. As a universal rule, if one relaxes, there is a tendency of floating in the water unless there are heavy tides or high currents in the water. In the same way, if one relaxes one's mind or spends some time in at least short meditation, there will always be a possibility that one can get some solution to the problem that one must be undergoing. In simple terms, by just getting worried, problems are not in any way going to run away, and in fact, will get enhanced by our worried and it will cause deterioration of physical health also.

Seek advice: One thing that we must understand, one cannot possess complete understanding or full knowledge to everything. We must help each other and seek an expert advice. There are billions of people around in the world and there are many good people who, perhaps is willing to help each other and to help you to choose right career and help you to come out of your tough situation.

Think ahead: Lateral thinking and thinking ahead of time are very important elements that we must follow. Thinking beyond the walls is very important. Updating ourselves is very good thing plus understand the future needs and act accordingly because it gives you lot of scope for better earnings.

Allow the money to earn money for you: At certain point of time or sometime in the future, we must allow the money to earn money for you. It is like allowing the money to bring and fetch more money for you. It happens only if you take proper financial advice from experts. Investing into better funds, saving schemes are very important things to consider and must understand the market fluctuations wisely. Plan appropriately for future necessities and needs. Financial advisors give wise advices, that is,

Do not invest into something that you do not understand. Just because someone has told you that this thing is good to save the money into, but its better to be cautious because it might fail you and you do not really anything about it. Try to invest in long term funds, which will definitely fetch you good returns because a good tree always take a long time to grow and gives good fruits in the long term.

Money is not evil as religion says: Since childhood, many of us are taught that money is evil if we are born and brought up in religious families. We are taught in such a way that GOD does not like money, but we need to think from practical aspect because money is not bad, it is all how we use it. For instance, phone is bad if we do not use mobile phones for good purpose and in the same way, any product or anything that we need to use. Money is needed to live a better life and is needed to live a comfortable life.

Buy experiences: Experience is very expensive because it involves lot of time. As far as I know, time is the most expensive element, though we can get it freely with no cost at all. For example, if you are writing an exam and preparing for exam and you do not have time to prepare well and as a result of which you were not able to exam. You must have wished, "I wish I had time to prepare well for exam". Learning is something that takes a bit of time to learn and life through time gives an experience and trying to understand that experience is always an expensive thing. There are lots of books available in the market, videos and so on to learn many things and moreover, we have internet, which is the biggest source of learning and understanding that experience.

Positive thinking: Think positive always, never, never, never feel jealous of others or feel led down just because someone is better than you financially. Many people think of giving you advices just because you are struggling a bit financially. Theoretically speaking, advice is very easy to give, it is like giving free advice, but truly speaking, no free lunches. We have earn those lunches ourselves.

Never give-up: There is always a tendency of giving up on things that we have been trying so hard just because it does not give us good results and/or its not happening. We must keep trying for better ways of achieving and some day, when the time comes, great success will come in whatever work that we do.

<u>Beware of a wolf in sheep's clothing</u>

On a daily basis, we come across so many people, and basically speaking, everyone possesses elements of positivity and negativity. Without one's knowledge, we crisscross both negative and positive elements. We bathe in the waters of negativity and we think that we are right always by pulling others down or being pulled by someone and we feel very bad about it, and later on, thoughts of revenge keeps swirling our minds, which is always a negative intention.

There is a nice story that I can narrate here to be simplified as dangerous people who is always walking besides us. Suppose, a person is staying in a building, with full of lighting, glory and honour, and unexpectedly, all of sudden, there is power loss, electricity cut happened. This person lit the candle and there was light, and hence, he decided to go ahead and give light to everyone. So, he started giving light to everyone. After giving light to few people, he gave light to another person, who is full of negativity. This person after taking the light, put off the candle who gave the light to him.

Likewise, there are so many people around us, walking besides us, saying sweet words and they behave like they cannot live without us, but I can guarantee that they are the most dangerous people on earth. They continuously keep backstabbing us without our knowledge and by the time, we are aware of it, already half of the damage is already done. These kinds of people do praise us directly and indirectly, but inside of their minds and heart, volcano keep burning out and unimaginable lava keeps boiling and would keep planning continuously on how to put you down when appropriate time comes. These kinds of people are very, very dangerous. People who attack directly are in fact, somewhat safe to deal with because their emotions are always directly expressed, so, bit less dangerous to deal with.

The society is full of negativity, must learn how to protect yourself from negative energy always.

People all around us and including us, filled with both positive and negative vibrations. Without our knowledge we do harm to others and we wear the face of goodness. It is like we always wear the sheep's skin

We always get the feeling that everyone is settled and we are still lagging behind, still struggling for money and living.

Must feel and experience life as complete..........

How to reprogram your brain

We all love to listen to stories. Age is not constraint to listen or to tell the story to someone. Story is always interesting because it deals with unknown elements, with new truths intermingled with fiction. We like to listen to stories because they contain supernatural elements plus they beautify and color every moment in the story so nicely that we would always wish to have that story life. Stories of flying horses, birds that carry us from this side to the other side, animals that talk to us, man marrying beautiful woman, all these elements are painted so beautifully in every story and we too would wish to have these elements in our lives. This is the reason why, we get attracted to stories. So, the question should pop up, why so beautiful life in only stories and why not in real lives. I believe, we should make some alternatives to our thought process to make things happen. Happiness is the main root of every one's life and it should be the reason for a healthy life. In the words of Aristotle, "Happiness is the quality of the soul…. Not a function of one's material circumstances."

So, in short, every human person has the right to write his/her own story. One can design life accordingly. This sounds funny as many say, life is a fate, what has to happen, will happen. No, it does not work like that, everything is your hands, how you want to live your life is entirely in your hands. Each one has been writing his or her story since birth with and without knowledge. As a child, without his knowledge, takes the role model of father or mother or anyone in the society and try to follow that particular person and imitates him and follows him and becomes like that person in the future. So, here, what he has done is, he has written his own life story of becoming that person.

Unknowingly, we chant correct or wrong mantras (feelings) and, accordingly create magnetic field of fortune or misfortune around us. Whatever positive or negative energies we feel around us, their waves have been created in the past by us. It is very important to realize the fact that nobody is decision maker in this universe except yourself. There is no power that decides your destiny; we create our own destiny. We alone are responsible for the rose flowers or the thorns that we have in our lives. God gives you a wild forest. You have to convert it into a garden. He gives you only stone and other raw material, you have to construct statues out of it. Therefore, we create our own reality. God neither beautifies nor spoils your life. He has slept forever after making the laws of nature. We hardly realize as to when we create negative energies through our thoughts and unknowingly attract misfortune. So, the seeds of misfortune are never sown.

At the time of birth, like animals, we have no samskaras (purificatory ceremony). Gradually, our mental and emotional actions-reactions start creating subtle waves of samskaras (purificatory ceremony) around our soul. After we die, the body gets destroyed but our thought and feelings, being subtle in nature, travel with our soul to the next birth and exactly according to these samskaras our nature, like-dislikes etc. are created. Our will power only alters their intensity. Destiny is the fruit of the seeds that we have sown and our actions (karma) represent our will power through which we strengthen a thought and sow new seeds which finally result in happiness or sorrow.

God neither decides nor is He interested in your destiny. You have to carefully sow good or bad seeds. It is your choice and your responsibility. If you want rose flower in your garden, you have to sow seeds of rose flower only. Saints and sages relinquish their family, business and society so as to remain free from these mental and emotional reactions. Whether you believe in God or not, does not matter because he decides nothing for you. It is your thought, feeling and emotion which will decide your future.

Whenever we face problems in life, our Gurus, astrologers inspire us to do prayers, worship and perform good actions so that our positive energies should increase thereby reducing our problems. It is a science of vibrations. Therefore, a person who leads his life in a pure manner and keeps sowing seeds of love, service and welfare, no power in this universe can affect him adversely.

Nothing is irregular in this world. Everything is governed by rules and laws. These rules and laws have been praised and upheld by our ancient sages and scholars. Since negative thoughts spoil the freshness of present moment, we should try not to repeat such negative feeling and thoughts. If you have an incompetent person in your house, office or society, do not discuss negatively about him because the more you discuss about his negative qualities the more negative vibrations are created around him thereby making it very difficult for him to improve. So if you want to improve a person and wish to see a positive change in him, always talk about his positive traits. It will, automatically, become a mantra for you and will create strong & magnetic positive vibrations around that person. You will surely notice positive changes in him after sometime.

Brian Tracy right said, "An attitude of positive expectation is the mark of superior personality" Here, the question is, how do we create our own stories, how do I write my life story and how do I get what I want... Always, visualize your future, like how you want your future to be, write it down in your personal diary, talk to yourself, and write down every detail of your future in your personal book and forget about it. Create positive thoughts and feelings and send that light energy into the future and that energy will take care of your dreams. There is always an angel or master, teacher, guardian, etc.. whichever the word you wish to use it. He or she is invisible, but always present and standing next to you. Remember, ask your master or teacher, whatever you need in life and it will be given to you. Visualize for things happening to you and it will come in right time for you. Always, one needs to develop positive vibration and culminate positive thoughts.

I wish to discuss further inputs, to start with, is the power of visualization. Suppose, for example, you do not have a house and need one. Now, sit in a comfortable position, deep take breaths and relax a few minutes. It does not matter whether you close your eyes or not, but will be better if you close your eyes and make sure you place yourself where there are no distractions, so that your visualization is really powerful. Upon closing your eyes, just focus on deep breathing only, inhale and exhale, and after a few minutes, imagine the kind of house you wish to have, either apartment or independent house, give it at least 3-4 years' time, visualize yourself moving into that house after that timeframe. Now, once you are done with this small exercise, make sure you pen down your thoughts about house in your personal diary, and in possible, be specific about the kind of house you wish to have in the future. Have a strong belief that you will be having that particular house at a specified period in the future and you can forget about it. To put in scientific terms, you have released positive vibrations or energy into the future and in turn, the cosmic energy also will make sure that your concerned thought is fulfilled, but one must have very strong believe and never doubt.

There are couple of things that one must do in order to increase positive energy and to stay away from negative vibration. Positive energy will indeed help one to build strong aura and positive power. One must block negative energy, if one feels oneself under any psychic or negative force attack from anyone; one must use his / her thumb to place a cross of blue light mentally on that attacker. One must be very strong and must face negative energy with positive energy and patient and must do it with sufficient will and power and negative energy will not reach you and will return to its sender. Always, one should direct good energy towards that negative energy.

Learn to develop your own magnetism, feel energy surrounding you as you walk, flowing through you as you converse with others. Expand it to other people in your vicinity and include them in your positive aura. The more you act as a channel of blessing to others, the more you yourself will be blessed. Your magnetism will be enhanced and your efforts to reach GOD (energy) greatly accelerated.

Spirituality is something that is not simply dedicated to spiritual gurus or religious people. Everyone that is living on this planet must become spiritual in order to live a healthy and happy life. At any time in life, one must be willing to meet some great guru in order to get some solutions in life. Here, I wish to discuss one secret, suppose, if I am not able to meet a great guru or Swamiji near me or by visiting any great places like Himalayas, one must not get discouraged. In that case, go to any temple or any place where is complete silence, now, close your eyes, and imagine a guru sitting in front of you and interact with him. One can get all the solutions to the problems that we face, but we must believe in this secret very strongly and things will indeed happen without any slightest doubt.

In order to face negative energy, there are certain things that we can do, they are, tantra, mantra and yantra.

Tantra – Since time immemorial, the term 'Tantra' has been used for a specific process, technique, method or a system like Bhairav Tantra, Dhyaan Tantra, Paak Tantra, Kaam Tantra etc. All healing techniques are Tantra skills.

All sorts of activities such as meditation, prayer, worship are actually Tantra skills. The use of a special method is called Tantra. The Tantra used with pure & selfless feeling is a 'divine Tantra" (White Magic) and the one used with ill feeling is called "Tantrikta" (Black Magic).

Yantra – Yantra is a geometrical shape or a design through which by using a special picture or lines, we express the force of powers & energies of the Nature and those of our own thoughts.   All these pictures, lines or symbol are called Yantra.

Yantra (symbols) actually help us to make our thoughts strong & powerful. An intention of wealth & fortune with Swastik surely yields better results as compared to the same intention without Swastik. Therefore, we need a symbol to empower our thoughts & intentions. Any symbol that once goes deep inside our subconscious mind immediately produces feelings associated with the symbol. According to this programming of the mind, Swastik implies a "pure & sacred symbol of beneficial energy" whenever you would see Swastik anywhere, your feelings would automatically, become pure & sacred. Now remove the four clockwise lines from this Swastik, thereby leaving just a plus (+) sign. Now when you look at it, your feelings would again change and you would start thinking about doctor/hospital because your mind has been programmed to understand that a plus sign in red colour means a doctor/hospital. As such, symbols have a tremendous importance because symbols form the language of our subconscious mind. That's why so many symbols have been formed till now. Now, if you show this Swastik to the Germans, they would look at you with hatred because a cruel and violent German dictator, Hitler had used reverse form of Swastik as his symbol. It only implies that no symbol has it sown power. It is the thought that gets generates on seeing that symbol which gives it the requisite power – negative or positive. No other religion, except the Hindu religion, has got any importance for Swastik. In other countries, Swastik is merely a good design and not a fortunate or sacred symbol.

Mantra – Mantra means a wave of a specific emotion or thought. Thought is generated from the mind and emotion from the heart. That's why wave of emotion is stronger than the wave of thought. So when we produce a specific emotion, a wave from our body forms a layer in our aura. When we produce this emotion repeatedly, these waves of emotion create a strong magnetic influence in the layers of our aura.   The kind of waves we generate through our emotions, similar waves of energy from the universe are attracted towards us. It is the law of Nature that Like attracts Like, means vibrations attract similar type of vibrations therefore, the actual meaning of mantra is that by repeating a feeling we created a magnetic impact in our aura and thus attract similar type of effect from the universe towards our selves.

Just like a tape recorder records our voice and the sound vibrations that we produce, similarly each vibration that we generate produces its signature in the aura. Our each vibration gets registered as an akashik record. Innumerable such vibrations are registered in the akashik records which have been successfully identified by precise instruments by modern scientists. These vibrations are permanently stored in the Universe & never get destroyed.

Feelings matter, and not language - We think, anything said in Sanskrit is a 'Mantra' or any language that cannot be followed is a Mantra. But the fact is that language has nothing to do with Mantra. Language is merely a medium. Primary thing is feeling. That's why hundreds of communities chant mantras in their respect languages and still get full benefit from it. Since the language of earlier times was Sanskrit or Pali, all the feelings, emotions, prayers were said in these languages only. The blessing in those times was like this – 'sarvebhavantusukhinah, sarvesantuniramaya' means everybody should be happy and healthy. Now, the same blessing is given in Hindi. The feelings/emotions are, however, the same. In earlier times, in case of any problem, people used to rush to God and pray in Sanskrit. The same is now done in Hindi language. Likewise, for different purposes, people had different types of prayers in Sanskrit. The same prayer is now done in Hindi or any other language of the devotee. One thing that is common to both the types of prayers is the feeling. But we have been made to believe that anything said only in Sanskrit is a Mantra.

So, in short, one must invite positive vibrations and strengthen one's aura and withdraw negative energy, and in a way, one must try not to look into the eyes of highly negative person or shake hands with him, which can have negative results.

There is no market for emotions

Being emotional is part of everyone's life. At one time or the other, many of us would have experienced some deep felt sentiments towards ourselves and towards others. Emotions are good and bad, in other words, they are neither good nor bad. Emotions are like a river that keeps flowing without one's consent. Each emotion is linked to another emotion. In other words, suppose, you fall in love or in love with a girl or a boy, there will be exchange of so many feelings among themselves. It gives rise to feelings of joy, grief, rage, longing, and jealousy and so on.

Now, with regards to emotions and feelings, though both sound alike, but they are different in meanings. We use and express ourselves in the words that we are comfortable with and at times, our body speaks rather than expressing through words. Many at times, we use words interchangeably to more or less describe the same thing as to how someone has made us feel. Basically speaking, emotions and feelings are closely related and they are like two sides of the same coin.

Emotions: Emotions are physical and responses of human body. Let's take an example, suppose, I am down with fever, body aches, then, my body would not accept being sick and would refuse to function normally. Suppose, I hit my leg on the stone by accident, then, it pains severely, human body does not accept the fact that it involved in a small accident in which body is experiencing tremendous amount of pain. Body reacts and there is so much swelling that is exhibited around the wound and bleeding also occurs. So, emotions are basically body's reactions to external stimulus. Anger, fear, surprise, disgust, joy and sadness are basic emotions that everyone experiences in one's life.

Feelings: Feelings are triggered and activated by emotions and are painted by personal experiences, beliefs, memories, and thoughts linked to that particular emotion. Think of someone or a teacher has hit the kid, and the reactions of the kid are pain that is seen and expressed on the face clearly. He or she shouts or cries in pain, which is verbal representation of those feelings.

Emotions and feeling is almost the same thing, but slightly different forms of expression like two sides of the same coin. Today, many movies and TV shows strongly display these emotions in order to attract many audiences, as in India, many of us are accustomed to these kinds of emotions. Suppose, one country is playing a game like cricket or football, and if you are the fan of that particular country, there is a strong sense of belongingness and oneness to support your country and the players. You keep reciting prayers in order that the players play well in order to win the match. When the team makes it up and wins the game after a long struggle, you will notice that there is an element of emotion that runs on your face in the form of joy, in the form tears and in the form of shouting. You will up all your friends and other people that our country has won the match and you will start declaring the greatness of the country.

Mental toughness: These days, its very important to learn the techniques of being cool in any given situations and circumstances. Basically speaking, it is very common for someone to react and express feelings. Suppose, someone has abused you and shouted you and illtreated you very badly, how do you react. Here, the question comes of handling that situation. Learning to be patient and learning to be positive and take things with positive attitude is very important. Suppose, even if you start reacting and start arguing, then, you have lost the battle and lost control of yourself. Balancing your emotions, I mean, not controlling them and you should never try to control your emotions, but they must be channelized in a healthy manner. By controlling emotions, it will create great devastating effects on human body and these emotions will keep bottling up and will one day blast out in the form of physical sickness or some psychological outburst. Suppose, in a workplace, someone has hurt you in some way or being shouted at for some silly errors, one should ignore these feelings and should continue to work as a group. It should not be like, as shown in movies, one should not think of taking revenge just because someone has hurt you and that is not correct.

Emotional intelligence: These days, emotional intelligence plays a vital role and is vey much necessary in today's world. People with emotional intelligence will be able to mix well and interact well with other members well and can work in groups without any problems. One needs to develop meaningful relationships with others, interpersonal skills and understanding, and must know their ability to manage their own emotions, and their personal skills.

Emotional intelligence is the ability to identify and manage your emotions, as well as other people's emotions. There are five features of emotional intelligence and they are,

Self-awareness is the ability to recognise your: emotions, strengths, limitations, actions and understand how these affect others around you and how to deal with them in a positive way. Identify your emotions and find a way how to handle them and manage your emotions and emotions of others. Try to analyse your strengths and weakness and use constructive methods to come to meaningful conclusions.

Self-regulation is managing your emotions. For example, if one of your employee makes errors, then, rather than shouting or firing that person, have a balanced mind and speak to that person positively because everyone including is capable of making errors, so, what is the point of losing temper just because he or she has made mistake or errors.

Empathy is your ability to understand other's emotions. In other words, placing yourself in the shoes of others. It helps you to understand others better and why they behave in a certain way. By being empathetic and exhibiting positive attitude, employees will develop trust and confidence in your and will perform job better.

Motivation is love towards your job. Love what you are doing without grumbling. When you love what you do irrespective of any job, it gives you greater satisfaction. It makes you focused on achieving more goals.

Social skills consist of effective communication skills and interpersonal skills that helps to build meaningful relationships between the members of the organization, and helps to develop trust and confidence in you. Employees will feel comfortable interacting with you and discussing many meaningful and innovative ideas.

So, being emotional about something does not help in anyways, hence, it is better to learn to stay positive, and by being positive, you will be in a position to exhibit your strong personality to people, no matter what the circumstances are.

How much stress is too much

Stress is anything that places a demand on us physically, mentally or emotionally. It makes us change the normal way we live. It disturbs human mind and our regular thinking and we falter and we cannot behave and think properly. Practically speaking, stress is always not a bad thing and most of us think that stress is very bad, but not all stress is bad. Without stress, I mean, astress, life would be boring. There would be no progress and no growth. For instance, if I have an exam tomorrow, then, some element of stress is needed, which is eusterss because it will help me to prepare exam properly and not take things for granted. Eustress creates seriousness and makes people disciplined about what they are going to do.

Eustress: Eustress means good stress. There are both positive stress and negative stress. So, eustress is a positive stress. To illustrate further, suppose, one is preparing for exams or is getting ready to play the match. The player is always a bit tensed as to how he would play the match. He knows he has practiced the match well and is ready emotionally and psychologically and physically, and even then, he feels a bit tensed about the match. This sort of stress is a good stress. It helps him not to take the match for granted and helps him disciplined. When he puts his feet on the ground and after 5 minutes of the play, all the stress will be disappeared. We have so many positive stress examples, like preparing to get married, planning to go for a vacation, and so on. During all these events, one feels and experiences certain amount of positive stress and excitement and thrill. It provides an opportunity to bring about positive changes in our lives.

Stress is the spice of life. Without stress, life would be boring. Productivity would decrease. Excitement in living would dwindle. We often seek out stressful, I mean thrilling experiences to heighten our sense of excitement. For instance, watching ghost movies, we know that horror movies cause certain element of fear and thrill, but we watch it for the sake of experiencing that thrill. Roller coaster rides are stressful, yet some people flock to them to have rides and experience thrill. Most movie plots center around the hero and heroine's attempts to get out of a conflict or stressful situations. Athlete talk of getting psyched up before a match to help boost their performance, and in fact, coaches and trainers create some element of positive stress in players in order to boost performance.

Stress: There is something called negative stress, which we are all aware of it. Experiencing tension, problems, all create negative stress. Stress brings about many physical and emotional changes. In general, one's body gets ready and gears up to meet a challenge. Some of the effects of stress are,

Physiological – pounding heart, rapid breathing, sweaty palms, cold hands and feet, lack of energy, headaches, muscle tension, sleep difficulties, stomach disturbances, etc..

Emotional and mental effects – irritability, nervousness, lack of patience, losing temper, worrying, emotional sensitivity, memory lapse, lack of focus and concentration, increase in careless errors, negative attitude, negative thinking, etc…

Behavioural – sleeping more, sleeping less, eating more, eating less, angry outbursts, withdrawing from others, drinking alcohol, smoking cigarettes, and so on.

My cup of stress: How a person copes and reacts to a stressor depends on their own constitution, temperament, past experiences, training, ability to handle stress and many other contributing factors. However, probably the two factors that most affect how we react to stress is how we perceive the stressor and our own ability to handle the stress successfully. For some, jumping out of perfectly good airplanes is extremely anxiety arousing. They doubt their own ability to cope successfully with this unnatural situation. However, others find parachuting exciting and thrilling. They may experience some fear, but do not doubt their ability to cope. Tough, realistic training is one of the best ways to help soldiers develop resistance to the effects of stress on the battlefield. It builds confidence and the soldier's ability to operate in a combat environment. When the stress is very high, it lasts long and some of the negative effects of stress are, depression, ulcers, headaches, hypertension, anger, irritability, weight loss or gain, fatigue, and so on.

Coping strategies: Keeping life in balance requires effort. It means watching where your time is spent and making a conscious effort to maintain a balance. If the demands at work are high, those demands need to be balanced by enjoyable activities, both at work and outside of work.

Break down every big job into small components, so it does not become overwhelming to you. Make a list of the work you want to accomplish each day. Prioritize your list and work on accomplishing the top three items.

Do neck rolls frequently throughout the day to relieve the stiffness and tightness in neck muscles. Let your shoulders drop and release the tension.

Become more aware of your surroundings. By deliberately slowing down your walk and conversation, your absorb more of your surroundings and reorient yourself to a slower pace.

Avoid being perfectionist. Put your best effort into whatever you are doing, then relax and do not worry about the results. Perfection implies unrealistic expectations. Perfectionists are hard to live with because of the excessive demands they make on themselves and others.

Temporarily, remove yourself from the situation when problems begin to overwhelm you. Once your mind is rested, you will see solutions.

Be assertive, take action and speak clearly and openly on your ideas and needs.

Take time out from your work, schedule regular vacations and opportunities to get away from it all. Try to plan these in such a way that they are long enough and frequent enough to allow you to relax and change your routine and pace.

Exercise regularly and moderately, research has suggested that those who exercise regularly, i.e. three to four times a week, tend to live longer and healthier lives than those who do not, walk, run, bike and play sports.

Maintain a reasonable diet, three meals a day is important for all of us. A number of research studies have suggested that those who have three meals a day live longer and healthier lives. Avoid junk food and try to eat a balanced diet. Listen to your body and its reaction to your food intake. If you attend to your body's reactions, you will learn the importance of regular and balanced meals.

Develop outside interests and activities, total involvement in job or home responsibilities can produce total isolation and monotony. Relax on weekends by doing something different from the pattern you have established during the week.

Think about something entirely different than work. Close your eyes and visualize an extremely relaxing and peaceful scene. Try to see it as clearly and distinctly as you can in your mind's eyes. Color in the trees and the ocean. Focus only on the color. Let yourself relax, let the tension slip away, take a deep breath and slowly.

Talk it out, when things get to you, find someone you can talk to and confide in. Expressing your feelings has a purpose. It allows you to release the feelings of tension and anger that you have built up. Effective communication with others is a key factor in being able to cope with stress. Keep the channels of communication open with those close to you. Learn to talk about your frustrations and thoughts.

Relievers

re are *101 Stress Relievers* on the next page to help you discover new and exciting
stress.

101 Stress Relievers

ANGRY? TALK TO A FRIEND ABOUT IT.
Apologize for a mistake.
Stand up and stretch.
Ask for help. CRY
Call up an old friend.
Build a model ship.
TELL someone "I love you."
STOP AND YAWN

Change coffee break to exercise break.

Close your eyes. What do you see?
Count to ten—or 1000—before exploding.
Count your blessings—make a list.
CLIMB A MOUNTAIN.
Cut back on caffeine
WATCH A REALLY GOOD MOVIE.
Plan ahead.
DAYDREAM spend your coffee break at the beach.
Do one thing at a time.
Eat a good breakfast. Forgive someone.
Fly a kite. Get a massage. Get a pet.
Find someone you're grateful to and thank them.
GO fishing. Play with your dog.
Get a good night's sleep.
Get up fifteen minutes early.
GO for a brisk walk. swimming to work a different way.
Hug a tree. Hug someone you love.
Keep a journal of thoughts and feelings.
Laugh at something you did.
Leave the car at home and take the bus.
Lie in a hammock.
Lift weights.
Listen to the birds
Make love.

LOOK at the big picture.
closely at a flower, leaf, blade of grass or tree trunk.
off into the distance.
Read a good book.
Make a list. Then follow it.
Take a child to the playground.
Take a deep breath and let it all out.
Take a leisurely stroll.
Take a long bath.
Take a nap.
Take an herb tea break.
Take one day at a time.
Take the back roads.
Take the stairs.
Take time for the sunset—or sunrise.
Take up knitting.
Play a round of golf.

WASH THE CAR. Plant a flower. Smell a rose.
READ SOMETHING FUNNY EVERY DAY.
Ride your bike to work.
Share feelings with someone.
a cat in your lap
on some music.
plants in your office.
your feet up
WEAR EARPLUGS WHEN IT'S NOISY.
WORK OUT AT THE GYM.
Massage your temples.
Quit smoking
Write a poem.
Write a letter to the editor.

around in a circular motion.
Sit by a fountain or stream. Close your eyes and hear the water.
Do a good deed.
TALK TO YOURSELF: "I CAN DO A GREAT JOB." "I CAN STAY CALM UNDER PRESSURE."
Paint a peaceful scene—in your imagination.
Write... down your fears down your dreams your congressman

Make time for play.
Spend an evening without TV
Sit by a fire.
SING A SONG.
Walk barefoot in the grass.

ICE YOUR HEAD AND STRETCH YOUR SHOULDERS

How to become a great learner?

Success is no accident. It is hard work, perseverance, learning, studying, sacrifice and most of all, love of what you are doing or learning to do.

What would you do if you were not allowed to get an education? You couldn't read or write. You had to work a minimum wage job at a factory and you weren't happy with the job. You couldn't teach your kid any skills because you didn't learn anything. Education like a torch light disperses darkness. Education is power, banishes ignorance, enriches and nourishes. Learning is a continuous process and we learn new things every day. The basic question comes to us why do we have to learn at all, what is the necessity of learning. We require food for survival of our physical body and for our nourishment, and thereby, we gain energy. We do not even realize that our mind continually thirsts for knowledge. It is human basic instinct that our mind will want to know more and more things. Our mind is inquisitive about knowing new things, new adventures, about new movies, new stories, and to what is happening around us, and perhaps, curious about new occurrences in the society and the world around us.

Albert Einstein remarked "Education is not learning of the facts, but training of the mind to think." There are so many things in this world that need to be learnt. Our mind only receives and can comprehend certain facts only. For example, when we read a book, we do not remember everything that we have read. We may not like all the arguments that have been printed in the book. Certainly, there are certain points that attract us, and we cherish them in our minds and pen them down in our diary or some other book that is precious to us. So, by studying, reading, and learning things, we are basically training and sharpening our brains to think more sharply. In the physical world, we need material things to fulfil our physical needs and we need currency to purchase them. Practically speaking, we cannot completely pile up material things or currency around us and keep consuming them. We just need them little by little as we live along. In the same way, our mind only grasps small quantities of knowledge at a time.

Up to the period of Renaissance, people were restricted to think and even curtailed their freedom to read books. They were compelled to read only a few books that were prescribed to them. Learning was a sin during the medieval period. During Renaissance period, people crossed the threshold of intellectual darkness and entered into the world of enlightenment, and explored various possibilities and methods of learning. By 20th century, people broke the barriers of conventional thinking, learning, and opened the doors to new ways of thinking, new ways of exploring, which made them free thinkers, and this is really an unremarkable accomplishment.

In terms of knowledge, there are so many things in the world that needs attention. There are so many mind-boggling questions in this world and universe that have remained unanswered. In fact, we have not even able to scratch the surface of knowledge that is present in this world and universe. Our mind can learn only certain things to certain extent. It is injudiciousness to think that we can learn everything in one day or to desire to want to know everything. For instance, is it impossible to drink a huge pitcher of water at once or to drink body of water from the river in one gulp. It is unquestionably impossible task to achieve. Once, St. Augustine was taking a walk on the beach pondering about creation, world, universe, God, and various other things. As he was walking on the beach, he noticed a small boy playing on the beach by digging a small hole in the sand, and then, he started pouring sea water into the hole. He continuously was fetching water and pouring water into the hole. Augustine was very curious about it and asked the boy as to what he was doing. The boy said that he was trying the empty the ocean. Augustine laughed at this and said that it was impossible. The boy then replied saying, "then, how do you think you can learn everything with your small brain." Augustine was puzzled about the answer, and the boy instantaneously vanished.

Education brings us reputation and value to ourselves. One becomes more valued in the society if one puts on the garment of learning and education. For instance, if we notice difference between learned and illiterate, whom do you think people would value more? Obviously, the learned gets primary significance and they are respected in the society than the illiterates. People think that they have better knowledge and well informed of many things of the society and the world. Gold and diamonds are considered as precious metals because they are more valued in the world market today than silver or other metals.

Education is not all about studying and getting good marks. It is really a means to discover new things, which we don't know about and increase our knowledge. An educated person has the ability to differentiate between right and wrong or good and evil. It is the foremost responsibility of a society to educate its citizens. Education helps man to make right choices at the right time. A person becomes perfect with education as he is not only gaining something from it, but also contributing to the growth of a nation. We must realize the importance of education. We must aim to ensure that each citizen of our nation is educated and independent.

Nelson Mandela said "Education is the most powerful weapon, which you can use to change the world." Education dispels darkness. Being illiterate or lack of education will only bring disaster in life. If we were to walk through a dense forest, what do we do, we at least carry a small torch light to disperse the darkness to move ahead. Otherwise, we might find it extremely difficult to go ahead unless there is providence of moonlight, which we cannot expect in every situation. Revathi is an illiterate woman and her son is highly educated, both of them are living in a remote village. Her son after completion of his studies goes back to the village to see his mother and stays with his mother for some time. One day, the son goes out to attend to a small business of his own. Revathi in the meantime prepares food for his son by using firewood and some waste paper, which is found in her house. After sometime, son comes home and tells mother that he has got a good job in the city, and he says he has to attend the interview. Mother is very happy about it. Son in the meantime searches for his certificates, but he is unable to find them. So, he began to worry about it. Finally, to his astonishment, he finds pieces of burned papers near the wood-burning stove where his mother cooked food for him earlier. He felt devastated and ransacked because those pieces of burned papers are his original certificates. His mother's ignorance jeopardized his career.

Sarvepalli Radhakrishnan said "The end-product of education should be a free creative man, who can battle against historical circumstances and adversities of nature." Learning and education must help us fight against adversities and must make us more cultured human beings. We must nurture and develop right attitude. We can better handle many circumstances, situations, problems in the society if we have logical pattern of thinking. We need to use our learning in a fruitful way, so that it benefits us and the society. When we consume food, our physical body receives food and energizes our body and gives us strength. Likewise, education must energize our thinking pattern to act wisely and prudently, and at the same time, respecting and valuing other's opinions and thoughts.

Learning is a continuous process. It does not end when we complete our degrees. Our life is the process of learning until we take last breath. Socrates for instance was imprisoned and was about to be sentenced to death. While in the prison cell, he heard a companion singing a new song. Socrates was mesmerized by this song, hence, he wanted to learn this song and requested his companion to teach him this song. Grammarian in Robert Browning's dramatic monologue for example, kept learning until his last breath. In short, we must develop correct attitude to learn, which is very essential for us. It is bridge from ignorance to light, from darkness to the world of truth and enlightenment.

Reading books and literature, or any other books makes us wise and intelligible, and thus we are better informed about many things. Reading and comprehending author's concepts and ideas can be considered as the most intellectual intimate relationship. Through reading, one can explore into another person's mind to comprehend his or her thoughts. One can understand his or her mind emotionally, physically, spiritually, and in whatever way possible. The most closet and intimate relationship one can have is only through reading because through reading, one can understand another mind through their writings and literature, and in fact, one can enter directly into their minds. In short, authors and writers put down their thoughts, concepts, and imagination, both positives and negatives, and they capture them into a symbolic language using words that can be remembered, read, and understood for the future generations. It is really amazing that their imagination and wonderful thoughts of writings are still alive in the minds of people today and for generations to come, and writers are intellectually present today.

I strongly believe learning is important and valuable because without learning, the world would function more poorly. We will not be able to perform our routine activities appropriately. Learning in fact fetches us health, power, happiness, financial security, knowledge, and lot of other benefits. Knowledge gives us power and helps us in many ways to move forward in life, and hence, let us not cease to learn and help one another in climbing the ladder of learning. After completion of our studies and degrees, we must break the conventional pattern of thinking and develop our own pattern of thinking, and must present 'ME' to the world. When I begin to develop my own pattern of thinking, I believe that is the success of my own studies and learning.

Learn to enjoy every minute of your life. Be happy now. Don't wait for something outside of yourself to make you happy in the future. Think how really precious is the time you have to spend, whether it's at work or with your family. Every minute should be enjoyed and savoured.

Learning is a lifelong process and, in short, one should be passionate about learning new things every day. It in fact, helps us to live a better human life.

Information is power, wealth, and it is priceless

Information can mean many things, detailed information, factual details, stats, facts, data, figures, knowledge, whatever we call it, everything is information. Information is very valuable. Researchers spend so much of money in order to get small piece of information. For example, scientists like NASA or ISRO have made tremendous efforts to send satellites to the moon, just to obtain and procure some piece of information. Human nature and mind is so inquisitive that it searches for knowledge. I mean, lets say, someone is narrating a very interesting story, and he has narrated the story half way and left the suspense in the middle. Now, perhaps, the storyteller might have some urgent work, so, he decided to go, but the listeners cannot wait that long and will force him to complete the story in order to know the full story. This is the method people used to use in the past before movies came into being. A few centuries back, writers used to pen down interesting stories in the form of novels and leave a suspense line, so that, when the writer writes the next book, he can complete the suspense and will have good business because many people will purchase novels in order to get the truth behind the story.

Inquisitive Mind: Human mind is so inquisitive, it cannot sleep without knowing things, though we say, its okay, even if you do not wish to reveal to me, but later that same person will come requesting for information. Lets take an example of some people on a daily basis, lets say, neighbours, they are so inquisitive about their neighbours. Suppose, any bad occurrence or incidence has happened or good things have happened in the neighbourhood, people are so eager to know as to what has happened. This is because some people have designed their minds in a such a way that they need to hear some sort of news from people, otherwise, they will not get sleep.

Highly encrypted information: Data encryption translates data into another form, or code, so that only people with access to a secret key (formally called a decryption key) or password can read it. The purpose of data encryption is to protect digital data confidentiality as it is stored on computer systems and transmitted using the internet or other computer networks. Companies and some people make sure that their data is highly secure because for them, the data is very important and that is the reason why, they secure the data in some form or the other.

Role of hackers: Hacking is an attempt to exploit a computer system or a private network inside a computer. Simply put, it is the unauthorised access to or control over computer network security systems for some illicit purpose. They try to target the weak points of the computer and steal the required information that is needed for them. These hackers need information for personal gains and for professional gains. On a personal level, they perhaps need money and on a profession level, they try to steal information in order to sell that information or data to someone at a higher price.

Information is very expensive: Let's take examples of scientific experiments or archaeological excavations, which are very expensive adventures. When it comes space experiments, space centres or agencies from each country has conducted so many missions by sending satellites beyond earth in order to procure valuable information and each satellite would coast around millions of dollars. Scientific experiments would never stop, even though they are pretty much expensive, its only because human mind wants to know what is beyond the earth and of course, it is a way of protecting ourselves from any dangers that may occur from space. In order to validate that information is very expensive, I wish to give another example, that is, lets assume, someone has gained knowledge in stock market and he has gained so much knowledge and he knows how to gain money easily from the market. He has gained this much experience because he has put lots of efforts into learning and by trials and errors. Now, if someone new who wishes to learn from him, approaches him, so, will this experienced person teach him straightaway. My answer will be, no. He will definitely charge him with huge amount of money because his experience is very expensive, experience means knowledge and knowledge does not come free as there are no free lunches today anywhere in the society. We can never get anything free in this world, we need to purchase everything including food, water, knowledge, education, etc... for a price. This is the reason why, knowledge is very expensive and people do indeed spend huge amounts of money gathering information and knowledge and we cannot easily get it.

Internet, ocean of information: Internet is the biggest source of all resources today. If someone wants to learn something, one can easily learn by browsing certain websites and some videos that are readily available online. All the basic and advanced courses are available online today for free and some courses are paid courses. One thing one must be aware of is that, there are people who keep uploading wrong information, that is why, one must be in a position to judge which is correct information and which is wrong information.

As far as I am concerned, internet has nine levels, and in normal scenario, one cannot easily get access to all these levels of internet

Level one, is common web level where everyone has access to and does the browsing.

Level two is web surface web, and examples of these are reddit, dig, temp email services, new grounds, vampire freaks, foreign social networks, human intel tasks, web hosting, college campuses.

Level three is web bergie web, FTP servers, google locked results, honeypots, loaded web servers, jailbit porn, 4chan, rsc, let me watch this, steams videos, bunny tube.

Proxy is required after this point,

Level four, web deep web, on the vanilla sources, heavy jailbit, light CP, gore, sex tapes, celebrity scandals, VIP gossips, hackers, script kiddies, virus information, suicides, raid information, computer security, super computing, visual processing, virtual reality, etc..

Tor required after this point,

Hacking groups ftp, node transfers, data analysis, post date generation, Microsoft data secure networks, shell networking, cosmologists/MIT

Level five, web charter web, hardcandy, onion IB, hidden wiki, candycane, banned videos, banned movies, banned books, questionable visual materials, personal records, line of blood locations, assassination box, headhunters, bounty hunters, illegal games hunters, rare animal trade, hard drugs trade, human trafficking, corporate exchange, multi-billion dollar deals, most of the black market.

Closed shell system required after this point

Location of atlantis, josefmengele successes, crystalline power of metrics, AI in a box, geometric algorhythmic shortcuts, the law of 13s, etc..

Level six, the marianas web.

Level seven, intermediatory between marianas web and levels 7 and 8

Level eight, the fog/virus soup

Level nine, the primarch system, which is impossible to access directly, perhaps, our present day computers do not have the compatibility to access this level of internet.

Google: I have everything. !!

Facebook: I know everyone. !

Tweeter: I know what you guys think!!

Internet: Gosh!!! without me. !! you guys are nothing!!!
In fact, internet is the biggest source of knowledge if used

properly and if misused, its biggest hurdle to progress. There are always pros and cons in everything and it all depends on how one makes use of things.

How to make a sound decision?

What exactly is the power of suggestion?

It is when you think what you have heard and read are the same but they are not!!!!!

Example:

Please pour me a drink of water from the picture on the table.

Please pour me a drink of water from the pitcher on the table.

He is a picture in the major league.

He is a pitcher in the major league.

The above 4 sentences are perfect examples of the power of suggestion, which we may just miss because we are not utilizing our lesson covered on critical thinking. With SR, you have a job in front of you and you are proofing, have you ever run across a job where you believed you heard the dictation correctly and then upon relistening realized you did not hear what you thought you did? Sure, we all have. This is the power of suggestion.

The same holds true when you just cannot get a word and you are asking for help. Sometimes it is better to not let the other person know what you are hearing because then they have the power of suggestion in their minds. They need to use their critical thinking and listen to the voice file for their opinion without input on your thoughts when in doubt. This happens to me often. I will be the first to admit it. Sometimes it is just best to get up and walk away from the computer for a few minutes and you would be amazed that when you come back you hear something totally different than you heard the first time. Remember don't get frustrated, walk away for a few seconds for clearing of your head. Research, but don't spend too much time. It is critical for you to utilize your reference materials, but not to spend too much time researching. Remember complete the whole document when transcribing before beginning to look for even the first blank.

This is all about become an attentive listener. We all are guilty of making mistakes. Let's face it, we are not perfect, and these dictators sometimes don't make it any easier, but we have got to learn to become attentive and focused on our work. It is so important to be completely focused on your work when you are transcribing or doing SR work. The distractions are many which could come your way. Just a few examples:

1.   The family thinks mom or dad works at home so they are always available.

2.   The extended family wants you to run errands because they feel your job is not really a job because you are home.

3.   The phone rings and it is a salesman or somebody wanting to talk to you about an island in Hawaii or a vacation.

4.   The doorbell rings.

5.   Your friends call thinking it is a good time to just chat.

This has happened to all of us. This is when we become inattentive listeners. We need to remember that our concentration needs to be on the task at hand to utilize your best abilities while producing.

Educating the family and friends is a tough one. My suggestion is to just be blunt and tell them, you have a job and you have to do it. Tell them your hours and make them aware of when you are available to chat. I can tell you I had to do the same thing and I have been doing this for over 15 years.

The second thing is if you have caller ID, utilize it. Remember those calls which are unimportant or not urgent can be taken after work hours or never if you like.

The doorbell. Well, there is nothing we can do about this. We have to answer the door, but I will tell you a funny story when I first came to this team. One of the supervisors was on the phone with me. My doorbell rang and it was the UPS man. I went to the door and because they are here so often as I am an internet shopper, they wanted to talk. I was on the phone and I told them I was sorry but I needed to sign and get back to work. To this day forward, this UPS person, who is the same exact one who is here every time now realizes that I don't have time to chat before my shift ends and will leave my packages at the door and not even ring my doorbell. This is just an example.

Distractions can take us completely away from our critical thinking as well as attentive listening and thus we make careless errors. We always need to proof, but we may not have anything to correct in proofing a second time if we were giving all we have to the first round of listening.

We are all susceptible to the Power of Suggestion! It is just how we handle these issues which makes us successful or upset because of some dumb mistake which causes us to fail a report and thus making the client unhappy. The examples below are examples of the power of suggestion prior to editing.

The first column lists what the SR transcribed; the second column is what should have been transcribed.

Points to remember: Listen and read the report for the context of the document to avoid the power of suggestion.   Pay close attention to those wonderful ESL dictators. Most of the time words do not stand alone. Relate them to the document for quality.

If you obsess over whether you are making the right decision, you are basically assuming that the universe will reward you for one thing and punish you for another.

The universe has no fixed agenda. Once you make any decision, it works around that decision. There is no right or wrong, only a series of possibilities that shift with each thought, feeling, and action that you experience.

If this sounds too mystical, refer again to the body. Every significant vital sign- body temperature, heart rate, oxygen consumption, hormone level, brain activity, and so on- alters the moment you decide to do anything... decisions are signals telling your body, mind, and environment to move in a certain direction." (reference from Deepak Chopra, The Book of Secrets: Unlocking the Hidden Dimensions of Your Life)

I've been intrigued by this question of whether we could evolve or develop a sixth sense - a sense that would give us seamless access and easy access to meta-information or information that may exist somewhere that may be relevant to help us make the right decision about whatever it is that we're coming across.

Decision making is always a tough thing when we are placed in certain sort of situations and circumstances. We always believe and would try to not hurt others with our decision, but at times, it indeed happens, for which we have no control of. We must always think wise and act accordingly, which can in fact have lesser evil effects.

My problem is bigger than yours

Stress, tensions, depressions, problems affect all of us in every area of our lives, whether being a manager or labourer, secretary, supervisor, employee, executive, at home or at work. We spend 60 percent of our waking time at work. All of us know that our work does not stop when we leave our place of duty. There is a house work and the children to take care of. A parent that chooses to stay at home to take care of the house and the family will often report their time being spent at home 24 hours of the day and experience stress of wasting time and not doing anything.

All of us are different. We have different strengths, abilities and stressors. We also differ in the support system, family, support groups, friends, colleagues, that we have available to help us cope with stressful situations and environments. All these effect the way we react to tensions and problems and our ability to cope with the consequences of these problems. A senior leader may appear to have greater stressors, but he or she may have more resources available to cope with those stressors than someone less senior. The sources of workplace stressors can vary and they are, for example, role conflict, role ambiguity, work group relations, supervisor performance, overload, heavy work, feedback, frequent disagreements, demands and pressures and so on.

Generally speaking, workplace stress can be listed as,

Lack of control over the work and workplace.

Presence of uncertainty.

Existence of dysfunctional conflict.

General task and work demands.

These are the basic elements that can disturb positive environment and positive work culture. Improving workers' skills at coping with problems may prove initially beneficial, however, reduction in the negative effects of workplace stress in all four areas can only be achieved by management and employees working together to develop effective stress management policies and programs.

We know that work can be stressful. In some situations, we do have to grin and bare it. We get physically exhausted with stressful situations and heavy work, though if taken on a positive note, it brings out best performance from us.

Usually speaking, individual differences influence what stressors and problems we bring to the workplace, what we view as stressful and how we respond to stress. Stressors also come from job demands, such as long hours, high workload, and frequent deployments. These job demands require either adaptation on the part of the worker, changes in policies and procedures, however, there are other sources of workplace stress that cannot be tolerated. These include violence in the workplace, sexual harassment, and unsafe work conditions.

Social support serves as a stress mediator. If one's spouse is supportive, then, one's ability to cope with stress in the workplace increases. If there is a high degree of unit cohesion, more stress can be tolerated than when a unit disorganized and co-workers are not supportive of each other. Superior support, at least for me, may play a more important role in moderating stress than does spousal or family support. At workplace, stress has individual and organizational outcomes. The effects of high levels of stress or stress continuing over prolonged periods on the individual can be emotional or psychological such as depression or anxiety attacks. They can result in behavioural consequences, such as difficulty getting up in the morning to aggressive verbal and physical behaviour.

Effectiveness of stress varies on the extent of stress one experiences, such as,

Length of the stress: Too much stress or stress lasting too long can cause a decrease in the ability to do work. The clearest example is stress from lack of sleep. Research has shown that four hours of sleep is the minimum required for sustained operations. Lack of sleep causes severe drops in judgment, problem solving and the ability to work. In short, work related stressors may lead to accidents, illnesses, complaints, grievances, conflict with co-workers and/or decreased quality of work. From the point of positive element, some degree of stress is helpful and needed to improve job performance, learning, attention and concentration. For instance, the best defence against developing combat fatigue is tough and realistic training. If training is not stressful enough, then, self confidence decreases, learning and physical conditioning are hampered and necessary survival skills are not developed.

The right combination of intensity and duration of stress leads to optimal performance. Runners improve their performance by the appropriate mix of road work and speed work and short and long workouts. This dynamic stress is called inverted-U.

Office climate: The climate of the organization sets the tone for the amount of stress experienced by individual members. Working in an environment where personal needs and feelings are considered will decrease the amount of stress in the workplace. Whereas, in organizations, where people distrust one another and back biting is common, the stress levels greatly increases.

Extent of ambiguity in one's job or directions: For most people, uncertainty is a stress. When there is uncertainty at work, productivity will suffer. For instance, reductions in the force, job changes, changes in supervisors, decreased interest, worries for tomorrow and so on. Clearly defined jobs and roles lead to enhanced performance. It is easier to hit a target you can see than one you cannot see. When people see what is expected of them, they can better judge their own performance. It also becomes easier for a supervisor to rate a subordinate's performance. Lack of clear direction or guidance increase employee's ambiguity and stress.

Support from managers and supervisors: Manager support plays a critical role in reducing stress. The manager is in a unique position to either increase or reduce many of the stressors experienced at work and not just by reducing workload. A leader should consider adjusting workload to maintain the optimal mix of duration and intensity of stress. However, even without changing workload, the manager can buffer the effects of stress by providing information, support and esteem.

Qualities of a good manager:

One who listens and understands

Supportive

Visionary

Goal oriented

Flexible

Caring

Decisive

Team player

No favouritism

Teacher

Mentor

Good sense of humour

Communicator

Trusted

Humble

Acts as a buffer between demands and employees.

Signs of positive environment:

Workload is shared by all.

People are free to talk about problems and explore constructive alternatives.

Factors such as ability, sense of ownership, workload, timing and team development determine who makes decisions. Complaints are handled positively.

There is noticeable sense of team play in planning, in performance and in discipline, I mean, sharing of responsibility.

The decisions and opinions of team members are respected.

Collaboration is freely encouraged. People readily request the help of other and are willing to give in turn.

When there is a crisis, people quickly band together to work until the crisis is solved.

Differing opinions are considered important to decision making and personal growth.

There is a great deal of on-the-job learning based on willingness to give, seek, and use feedback and advice.

Relationships are honest. People do care about one another and do not feel alone.

Leadership is flexible, shifting in style and emphasis to suit the situation.

People are turned on and are highly involved by choice. The workplace is important and fun.

Risk is accepted and valued for growth and development.

People are free to learn from honest mistakes.

Frustrations are handled positively and openly.

A lot of energy is devoted to developing and clarifying standards. There is a sense of pride in attaining goals.

Signs of negative environment:

Counselling is avoided.

People feel alone and lack concern for one another. An undercut of fear exists.

People feel locked into their jobs. They feel stale and bored.

The leader is dominating and bossy.

The leader tightly controls new ideas and demands justification.

One mistake and you are out.

Poor performance is glossed over.

Innovation is not widespread, but consolidated in the hands of a few.

People swallow their frustrations, like I can do nothing, it is the responsibility of the leader to save the ship.

Standards are not clear, are often misinterpreted and do not seem to relate to important organizational concerns.

People are afraid to talk openly about problems.

Egos complicate problem solving. People treat one another in a formal and polity manner that mask problems.

Leaders feel along in trying to get things done. Somehow orders, policies, and procedures do not get carried out as intended.

People compete rather than cooperate. People distrust one another and back biting is very common.

Wolfin sheep's clothing. A dangerous person who is pretending to be harmless; an enemy who is disguised as a friend.

Conflict is mostly hidden. Arguments drag out and frustration grows.

Learning is difficult and they get little feedback on performance and must of that is not helpful.

Countering stress: There are many ways, organizations can work to reduce problems with workplace stress. In many cases, stress is inevitable. However, stress and workplace demands need to be offset by positive programs and policies. Take sailing for example, it is the balance of force that makes the boat move. The wind blows against the sail, but without the pressure of the water on the keel and hull, a sailboat would slide across the water and lack direction. Some of the ways, one can work out in dealing with stress and they are,

Taking a vacation

Physical activity

Fair rewards

Creating good environment

Build self esteem

Facilitate the work

Process and goal and so on.

Developing the right attitude

Attitude reflects in everything you do and everything that happens to you. The law of attraction is basically a concept which explains that you attract what you think of the most, so whatever you put out comes back to you. If like attracts like, positive attitudes attract positive events and people into our lives. This is why we must learn to develop a positive attitude in everything we do. When we adopt positive attitude, it is like setting a clear path for positive outcomes.

Your friend: In order to make your attitude your friend, you have to learn how to transform your attitude, so you can create the life you have envisioned and imagined. You also have to learn how t keep the best attitude possible most of the time as well as how to implement the idea of having a positive attitude throughout your life. It can take some work to transform your attitude and even to maintain it, but it is well worth it. Attitude is a hypothetical adopted state that reflects the like or dislike of an event, person or item. This means that when something is not going our way, we are prone to develop a pessimistic view, a negative attitude. This basically means that when things are indeed not going the way you would like them to go, you can train your mind to become aware of the negative state and transform it at will and it is possible. The key factor here is becoming aware of the mood and attitude that we are experiencing and consciously realize that with that kind of an attitude things are not going to magically change. However, when we do change our attitude, we may indeed see the situation change even before we start doing anything. This happens because we adopt a positive attitude, our mind opens to more possibilities and outcomes. Making your attitude your friend, means, choosing what that friend is going to be.

Your attitude is the way you act, think, and treat those around you, thus, it can be your helper, your friend. Moreover, your attitude affects everything in your life and builds a path as you go. Therefore, it greatly affects the way you think and how others treat you. Thus, it affects your path in life. Then, to make your attitude your friend means to let your attitude guide you on your path as well as act as your friend or contributor. Your attitude will then shape everything in your life. You are going to be travelling down the path, which your attitude lead you to. When you think positively, you will be less likely to see the negative in things and therefore, you environment will appear to change. It is the matter of perception. When you choose to adopt a positive attitude, you will most likely start to notice more than ever the little things that you used to take for granted and that will have an encouraging effect on you. You will start believing more in yourself, and as this self-confidence expands, you will believe that you can accomplish anything by just aligning your mind with it. You will be able to set goals and reach them because you will believe that you can do it. You will not have that negative energy to hold you back. A positive attitude is extremely powerful. It will start to share everyone and everything around you. You will be able to see the great power of this immediately.

Believe it: You must start by believing in the idea that you attitude affects your life and what happens to you. If you struggle with belief in the premise that when you think positively, positive things will happen, then the first step in making your attitude your friend is to change your way of thinking. You have to believe in the idea that positive attitude equals positive results. And when you consciously and constantly think of this premise, you will eventually believe it. To aid in your believing, you have to start looking for proof. There is plenty of room around you. It should not be hard to find out since positive influence and negative influence is all around all of us. You just need to decide to become an observer. Take for an instance, even by observing your bank teller or the grocery store cashier can give you some clues to determine how their days and lives are going according to their facial expressions, which talk a lot about their attitudes in general. Now, try it out for yourself. There is no better proof than experiencing it in the first hand. Take one single day and commit to having a positive attitude all day. Take notice of how others react to you. Once you have convinced yourself that your positive attitude really does influence your life, then, you can begin to put the idea of making your attitude your friend into play.

Checklist: Jus to put it out in clear terms, here is a checklist of what a positive attitude is and what it involves. Generally speaking, the main ingredient is developing the right mind-set.

Upbeat and cheerful.

Looks at the glass as half full and not half empty.

Can find the beauty in everything.

Thinks of the good before the bad.

Loves life.

Avoid negative words

May seem silly at times and uncommon in the eyes of people.

Loves to have fun

Never puts others down

Looks for ways to make others' lives better.

Can see the solution over the problem.

Willing to work towards goals

Ways to positive attitude:

Find a happy place in your mind and in your home. Create a place in your mind that is your ideal paradise. When you feel stressed or down, just go to your happy physical place. Then, go to your happy mind place, take a few moments to relax there and enjoy it.

Develop a hobby, do something you enjoy that makes you feel fulfilled. It will raise your spirits and allow you to maintain a positive attitude frequently.

Do exercise, while many people look at exercise in negative way, it really can bring positive influences to your life. When you exercise, your body releases endorphins, the happy hormones that act as natural pain relievers and give you a sense of well-being.

Practice affirmations, affirmations are phrases, versis or other short sentences that have a positive influence. Affirmations can be quotes, verses from the bible or other scriptures.

Explore new possibilities, instead of walking away from the unknown, be brave and courageous to walk towards it. In many occasions, you will discover something powerful to help you evolve and that will help build your positive attitude as you realize you can do it. Fear leads to negative attitude while courage leads to a positive one.

Do not walk away from a challenge, be brave and courageous. Allow yourself to accept challenges and try creative ways to deal with them. Problem solving is an art that we can all master, but as anything else in life, it requires practice.

Become a helper, the satisfaction we get just from the pleasure of helping others from the heart and without any personal gain or hidden agenda is one of the best experiences any human being can have. When you help others, you are helping yourself. You are contributing to your positive attitude because you are feeling useful to others.

Pretend, the imagination is a wonderful thing. Allow yourself to go to some make believe place, get away from your normal life and pretend you are someone else. Have fun and you are sure to smile.

While this experience can teach you about how your attitude can become, your friend or your enemy, it also teaches you to do everything possible to make sure your attitude is mostly positive. Once you start to live with the idea of making your attitude your friend, you will start to see changes, especially if you have been living with a negative attitude and have decided to change this.

Adapting a positive attitude and making it the path you travel through will impact your life in many ways. You are going to start to see the positive influence right away. People are going to start treating you in a more positive manner.

People will respond positively to someone who greets them with a positive attitude. Think of a time when you gave a stranger a smile. He most likely smiled back to you, that is positive attitude at work or outside. You can start using this attitude to influence people in many ways. As you start to adapt a positive attitude to your life, you will begin to be able to see the positive in everything that you can across.

Being daredevil

One should develop strong personality. We should not blink our eyes in times of difficult situations or circumstances, no matter what happens, and after all, what will happen, nothing, it will try to cause some damage to body or cause sickness and will go away. It will be like a cyclone or passing clouds that come and go. That is the reason why, never be afraid, one must be very strong and courageous. Suppose if you are standing in the pitch darkness, what will happen, many get scared as something or some ghost will come and eat you. Just because we dot see anything in the dark, it does not mean something is there or something is not there. We need to be brave. I still remember, years back, I had to cross the forest at night to reach my home alone. I knew, it was forest, no lights, it was almost a couple of kilometres and I know there are animals in the forest and in spite of this, I went ahead and walked courageously thinking, that nothing will harm me and in fact, nothing has happened. So, fear is basically that comes to us and says, I am standing next to you, but I will tell the fear to go away and I do not want you as my companion because fear is useless companion. Fear is not my emotion and it is the emotion of fear. So, why should I feel empathy for fear and experience that feeling as if it is mine.

Facing challenges: Life is full of challenges. Accept any challenge as they come to you even if you are new to them, face them with courage. Challenging situations often can come to anyone. It is not that one particular situation comes just to take a revenge. Usually speaking, people will have to face certain situations and those difficult situations will toughen them and make them stronger than ever. Fear is an element that keeps creeping as to how to handle any situation that they are faced with. Fear if we manifest in human form, is a devil that stands next to us. It seems that on most days and most of the time, we love this guy, fear, but we must keep this guy away and make sure we are completely free from him. We must be able to tell him, please I am not interested to invite you in my house or walk with me. We must make sure we make a strong decision to drive this fear from us because this fear is the biggest obstacle for progress.

Checklist:

Being honest and taking responsibility for your actions are admirable qualities.

Adaptability and compatibility are great traits that can help you get along with others.

Drive and determination will help you keep going no matter what.

Compassion and understanding mean you relate well to others.

Patience is a virtue and also a good personality trait.

Courage will help you do what's right in tough situations.

Loyalty is a good quality to possess, making others trust you.

Types of personalities:

Openness: appreciation for a variety of experiences, ready to explore adventures, new things and imagination.

Conscientiousness: planning ahead rather than being spontaneous. These types of people are organized and have a strong sense of duty. They're dependable, disciplined and achievement-focused.

Extraversion: being sociable, energetic, talkative, more of a social butterfly. They are more chatty, sociable and draw energy from crowds. They tend to be assertive and cheerful in their social interactions.

Agreeableness: being kind, sympathetic and happy to help. Disagreeable people are cold and suspicious of others, and they're less likely to cooperate.

Neuroticism: inclined to worry or be vulnerable or temperamental. This can happen due to dysfunctional parents. He worries about everything, and might quit a job because of his anxiety over not having access to a private bathroom.

Walking style: Your walking tells you about what you are and how you talk, think and behave. Walking exhibits your mannerism and your personality. Many people really do not bother about walking styles, gestures, body movements, and actions. They speak a lot about ourselves. Usually speaking, one must walk straight with head up with strong conviction and believe in yourself. You must be very strong in your thought and your walking carries you. When you speak, voice out, do not be soft when needed to speak out or be silent. In order to display good personality, walking style, being very bold, courageous, strong, being confident are all very important factors that we need to consider. In whatever situation you are in, make sure not to compare your skills with others because you are completely you, unique and no one can replace you and because you are very special. Do not insult yourself by ignoring yourself, by not giving sufficient respect to yourself. Never underestimate your skills and just because someone is very good and you think he or she is very good at studies or good at something else. We cannot and can never compare with anyone because it is like five fingers of the hand, which finger would say is better than other fingers and all are equal and strong and beautiful fingers. Your skills is very unique and no one can replace you, that is the speciality about you.

Be yourself: Make yourself a best friend, be yourself and never try to imitate others, why would you want to be someone. One thing we do not notice here is that, we spend most of the time with ourselves. So, try to communicate with yourself and make yourself your best friend and ask and be guided by your best friend. In life, we come across with many people in schools, college, colleagues, some turn out be good friends and some do not. If we develop positive attitude, we can attract right kind of people who would give us positive energy and boost to our present and future. We must have good circle of friends, even though in society, we will find, max negative people only. Next thing is, we have grown up since childhood by seeing, believing in something that we do not know. Suppose, for example, someone told me, GOD is present in temple or in church, how do you know that GOD is there only. Have you ever questioned yourself and/or gone beyond your believe system. We must go beyond text books that have studied, books that we read, question everything in order to find the truth, question the very existence of you, as to why you have come to this earth and what is the meaning of your life, we must do this with a positive attitude.

We have so much of knowledge in this world, given and contributed by others. The question is, why should be blindly believe in that knowledge, do your own research and you will definitely find answers. Another important thing is, whatever you are, fat, thin, dark, fair, etc... accept yourself as you are, love yourself and do not judge and compare yourself with others and if you try to compare yourself, you are insulting yourself. Past has nothing to do with our future. Future is in our hands. See the different possibilities. Program your brain, it is like neurolinguistic program, we can tune our minds and our brains. For example, washing machine is programmed in such a way that its duty is to wash clothes, that is it and it will not know other than washing clothes. In the same way, program your brain as to how you want to be, declare your future, I mean, design your own program, writer your own life story for future. Tell yourself constantly that you are going to have a beautiful life and have a positive attitude and things will come running towards you. For instance, especially for students, if someone tells you, you are a slow learner or an average student, would you agree. I mean, do not agree, who makes the rules for your body and mind, program your mind that you are genius, and only thing is put your efforts and increase your concentration and focus and I can tell you, you will come out with highest possible scores in your studies.

There is nothing impossible, but only if you try, the impossible become a possibility. Suppose, if someone asks you, how is this Sunday going to be, just be bold and tell them, it's going to be such a glorious Sunday, even though, you will have no chance of going out, so what, you could have accomplished many tasks that needed to be done at home. Decide what you want in life, it is not about dreaming or setting goals, for instance, you want to fly, make it happen or want to become a CEO of the company, become one and program your mind that you want to become one or have your own business. Once you reach that position, just say with strength and boldness in your voice and with confidence, it is not just because I dreamed, but I wanted to be in this position, so I am today.

Attitude: One needs to have right kind of attitude. There are always two ways of looking at life and at things. Suppose, you are waiting at the train station, waiting for a train, let's say, you are on time to catch the train and you hear the announcement saying that the train is delayed by one hour and again another one hour and again, another two hours. You have a situation of a late running train, so, what would be your reaction, here, there are two ways of accepting this situation, first, usual reaction is cursing the rail company for not maintaining the timings of the train, this is negative way of thinking and negative attitude. From the aspect of positive attitude, you will bless everyone and whatever happens, you would feel happy because perhaps, you have the time now to do your personal works by going into the town or complete some work on your laptop or read a book peacefully or observe people in the railway station.

As a thumb rule, always, keep climbing the ladder. If you think, learning is expensive, try ignorance, they you will know how expensive ignorance is. You must keep learning always and you must have passion towards learning because learning is money and we need to invest time in order to learn and learn from others.

Burned love in married life

In life, everyone is so excited about marriage. Boys and girls, during their college life, strongly wish to have boyfriend or girlfriend. Each one lives in a different worlds, a world of fantasy, world of dreams and nothing comes across or disturb their dreams. After achieving good job or business, one eagerly waits to get married and it does happen in everyone's life, unless one decides not to marry and live a celibate life for whatever reasons. In the initial days of marriage, everything is so beautiful, for boy, girl is an angel and she is everything for him and for girl, he is the hero, but these feelings do not last for days. After one year or two, all these feelings disappear and each one gets attracted to different persons, boy getting attracted to a new girl and girl getting attracted to new boy, and this is something very common. The reason as to why this happens, probably, each one knows that they are now married and there is likelihood that each one takes another for granted or perhaps, one does not keep themselves clean or with their negative attitude, can cause irritation to each other.

Marriage is a mutual understanding and a long-term relationship. Before even considering marriage, one must introduce one's prospective husband or wife in his or her field of business and social activity. Thus, you can to certain extent find out whether or not the prospective partner is in harmony with your habits or ideals and whether you can fit in with his or her ambitions, temperaments, ideas. Now, instead of constantly living and thinking only on the physical plane, I mean, looking at your wife only sexually, learn to love your wife or husband more on the spiritual plane and associate as close and best friends. Here, the thing is, man has his own vibrations, both positive and negative and at the same time, woman has her own vibrations. It is a combination of different vibrations, but here, the main point is, both must attempt to increase more positive vibrations, which in turn can help both of them to grow faster on a spiritual plane and this is the sole purpose of human life.

Routine Life: From the point of husband, he keeps seeing her daily and after two years of marriage, he gets used to her and even she does not even bother and takes things for granted. Now, here is the point, because of these mentalities, girl usually does not dress up well as she used to do before marriage and even boy also. As a result of this, at least on the level of physicality, attraction is missing towards each other and in turn, each one look at each other as enemies, though not externally.

Need of new girlfriend: Every husband definitely thinks of having a new girlfriend who looks charming, sweet, lovely, encouraging, confident, being positive, looks gorgeous, with correct fitness, etc.., but here, the question is, how does this happen to a married person. Very simple, stop looking at your wife as your wife, start considering her a new girlfriend whom you just have met, imbibe the kind of qualities that you wish to have in her, but do not command and do it lovingly. In the same way, every wife needs a new boyfriend and must be done the same way. It the perception that matters and how one looks at each other again with a fresh look.

Some love precepts:

Address your wife or husband as sweetie, babe, etc… with love and dignity.

Remember important dates and events of her or his life, especially birthdays, marriage anniversaries, etc.

Help to lighten the kitchen work with right kind of support.

Develop mutual interest towards each other.

Engage in uplifting discussions rather than negative and heated arguments.

Give your wife financial responsibilities and learn to spend money wisely.

Give her freedom to choose her women friends. Learn to respect and appreciate her friends.

Have a family meeting once in awhile, discuss various things and difficulties together and try to get some solutions.

Keep your body fit and eat healthy food.

Do not try to make your wife think that you are the owner of your wife's body or own her, but just make her feel that you are glad to have whatever she gives you from her soul.

Do not be jealous of your wife and make her miserable by nagging and never insult her parents nor allow her to insult your own parents.

Do not argue with each other, especially in front of other.

Speak highly about each other in front of others.

Try not to disturb your wife when she is busy with her work, either personal or professional and the same thing applies to husband also.

Every person needs a time where one needs to spend time in solitude, a way to self-realization.

Be a good friend, spiritual companion and after all, need to stay together until the last breath.

This rule applies to both – keep yourself neat, clean, attractive and well dressed, just as you first met him.

Have a special occasion where as a family, spend some time outing together or if possible, go outside as lovers once again on a ride, possibly long ride, which will help in turn to strengthen the relationships.

Unhappiness and disappointment with negative behavior with each other are the visitors that keep coming in married life. One must learn to gently say no to these visitors and must ask them to leave slowly, though may not be possible to shut them off at once.

Flying dreams

OH MY SWEET DREAMS.............

Words.... words... wow! you are so sweet, how!

With a basket of flavours and what a wonder,

you are so cool and large like ocean waters,

We have no container to hold and preserve,

My mind like a river has perennial flow of thoughts,

in my mind, you keep dancing like waves of ocean,

with so many abstract colours, feelings, questions and answers,

hmm, sometimes bitter, and at times, delicious to my mouth.

Me, standing on the hilltop, and gentle breeze touches my hair.

Goosebumps on my hands and thoughts twinkle like diamonds,

from dawn to dusk and birth to death, they travel, travel, and travel.

I try to dig out from my memory for words once I have learned;

like gold, they sparkle, and words sprout from my memory as i speak,

like dew drops, they shower and sprinkle pain and joy every second.

oh! what a flow, what a marvel, i wish i could fly like a bird and sing,

hmm, sometimes, they squeeze hearts, and at times, they soothe.

From hilltop, i travelled in time to the land of Iceland,

looked around, it is beautiful everywhere and snowfall from the sky,

Wow..wow.. wow.... whiteness all around me, with sweet smell of snow,

hu, hu, hu, hu. hu………. I am shivering, but my heart feels joy,

the air is freezing with cold and the snow is still drizzling,

'good morniiiiiigVizag..' words from radio mirchi touched my ears,

Snow, wind, where are you... oh my god, was i dreaming, what a sweet dream,

I wish the sweet dream may remain with me in my beautiful life.

Why do employees not take vacation

People these days, especially middle class and lower middle-class people keep working day and day out, and night outs to make a proper living. The cost of living keep growing like a mountain daily and prices keep increasing. Hence, many people find it really hard to pay the bills and run the house and are met with tension. As kids growing older, they have to think of paying school fees, books, family maintenance, house maintenance, and other expenses. So, there is very less scope for personal life and growth. Many of us in some way or the other are so occupied in trying to earn money and we are in fact forgetting ourselves.

There are so many holiday destinations like theme parks, beaches, children parks, temples, resorts and so on. Visiting some of the parks is quite easy because they are less expensive, but going to theme parks or resorts or taking a break from regular job and going to some outing is extremely difficult. Frankly speaking, do we really get a break from jobs these days, especially since most of us are working in private industry. Of course, given the fact that some are high salaries people, can afford to take a break because of their work schedule. I know a person who makes living by just working as a security guard, but hardly gets anything to run the family. Expenses are overpowering his salary and hence, in order to reduce this tension, he has taken up another job and works at night. In other words, he is into two jobs and he hardly gets any time to breathe. No scope for personal life and he just sleeps for a few hours a day and whenever Sunday comes, he just sleeps peacefully. Here, the question is, he does not have time to spend with his family, his son or daughter. Children on the other hand, are missing daddy in their lives. People, many like this are experiencing such a stressful life.

Holidays and festivals: Holidays and festivals are illusion because every company generally give holidays on festival days and some companies due to hectic work, instead gives employees option of working even on holidays, by giving double pay. In order to get that money, many even sacrifice those festive holidays. This is very common for almost every lower middle-class family members. They keep chasing for income in order to meet daily expenses and try to save the money in the form of fixed deposits or post office savings. I still really wonder and really, lot many people are missing their personal life, spending quality time with themselves, with their families, or spending some valuable time with Nature, which would in fact refresh their minds.

Unused vacation: Many people today are into the race of chasing money. Since some people are fortunate to have some properties left by their parents or grandparents, they have the privilege of enjoying that property, but in general scenario, chasing for money is quite common. In spite of working day and night, under so much stress, bearing patiently blessings from the bosses and daily tensions that are involved in job, money keep people motivated in spite of all these stressful factors.

Vacation and picnics: Walt Disney World Resort is located in Florida, Magic Kingdom Park, sea world Orlando, Disney land Paris, Universal Studios, Singapore, Gardaland, Italy, Pleasure Beach, United Kingdom, Alton Towers, United Kingdom, Disney's Hollywood Studios, Orlando, Walt Disney World's Magic Kingdom, Florida, Efteling, The Netherlands, Port Aventura, Spain, Legoland, Denmark, Tivoli Gardens, Denmark, Shanghai Disneyland, China, Wonderla, India, Essel World, India, Essel World, India are some of the theme parks around the world.

Visiting one of these theme parks are bit expensive, but I believe, its best place to spend some refreshing time.

Sick leaves: Sick leaves do in fact give some scope for relaxation, but human body is not happy with the discomfort that one experiences. In other words, one does not completely enjoy the full freedom of relaxation, and feeling of loss of pay or less going in the mind. This causes some discomfort and uneasiness in the mind and body.

In search of money: Life is so busy, busy, busy. Only as kids, they enjoy some sort of freedom, but as kids, they think, it is burdensome to go to school and do some studies, which they feel at their age. Here, the main problem lies when one grows and reaches a certain age, he or she is compelled to get into some job or the other. At this point, it not he that makes the decision for himself, it is the society, parents, relatives make decision and psychologically will compel him or her to do something in life and until then, these thoughts will keep coming from others. It is the psychological stress that one experiences until he or she is very rich enough not to do anything and has got plenty of money or business to look after.

Life is being happy and spending time with friends, loved ones, visiting someone, spending some time with Nature, beaches, or someplace where you can get relaxed. Always, keep yourself relaxed, take a deep breath whenever you feel stressed out, wear a smile without blemish, it will in fact shines like a bulb. Human body is a like bulb, though we do not see it physically, it is like bulb that shines like radium at night, hence, life has to be a happy one and whatever one goes through in life, it is just an experience.

This book is the collection of intuitive thoughts, which I have gathered over the years like little diamonds and pearls, they help everyone in every aspect of life, in our challenges, to get a fewer answers to the daily challenges that we face or come across. Filled with insights, every word is impregnated with deep rooted thoughts, and would connect to some aspect or element of our lives.

<u>With love and gratitude:</u>

<u>Joseph Leonardo</u>, the writer, the dynamic speaker, motivational coach, working as a Human Resource manager for over 20 years, and loving dad, lives in Visakhapatnam, Andhra Pradesh, India.

leonardojoseph16@gmail.com

deepeshjosephn@gmail.com

Joseph Leonardo